Married with Luggage

What We Learned about Love

by Traveling the World

By Warren & Betsy Talbot

Contents

in case everything came loose. Neither one of us had to say it out loud.

Warren donned his headlamp and knelt by the front door of the tent. We executed our well practiced "mosquito maneuver," a quick in and out of the tent while the person inside zips up quickly. We developed this technique in Scotland to keep the swarming biting flies called midges out. I never dreamed we'd be using it to fight blowing sand in a storm at the edge of a cliff.

Warren used a rock to hammer the stake in deeper and retie the flysheet over our tent. The wind was so strong I could barely hear him pounding the stake outside, but I could see the light from his headlamp. His light bobbed as he walked around the tent checking all the stakes and ties and placing big rocks over them. Satisfied, he called to me that he was coming back in. After a reverse mosquito maneuver to re-enter the tent, he gave me the rundown on the situation outside.

The wind was strong, and we had little protection from it in our current location. With the tent cinched down as tight as it could be, we had to hope it was enough. We lay back down and listened to the storm outside, wondering if we'd get any more sleep that night.

Our little analog travel clock sat in a mesh pocket on the inside of the tent. We'd purchased it on our honeymoon in Paris back in 2004. I remembered the rainy day we bought it, after a lazy afternoon of wine, cheese, and sex. We needed to get up early the next morning to catch a flight home, and the room in our quaint hotel didn't have an alarm clock. I flashed back to the feeling of those soft sheets on my skin, the sweet exhaustion of new love, and the comfort of that hotel bed. The grit in my sleeping bag ended the memory and brought me back to the harsh reality of the present. We were a long way from romance in that moment.

The glowing arms of the clock showed the time as 12:10 a.m., still a long way from sunrise. Neither of us expected to get any sleep, but fatigue won and we dozed off. The time was 1:30 a.m. when we woke up again, this time to the sound of rain pelting the tent. The storm was growing.

I pulled in our bags of food and hiking boots from the outer vestibule of the tent, further crowding our small space. My go-to move when I'm nervous is to nest, to pack myself in with my necessities as I face a problem. As I rearranged our space, we evaluated our situation. Our tent was perched on a cliff jutting out toward the Mediterranean Sea on the coast of Turkey. The wind was so strong it could blow our tent out to sea if we tried to take it down. The nearest shelter was in the village we passed late the day before, at least a mile away uphill and over rocky terrain. The rocks on the cliffside trail were already slick from rain and would be dangerous to walk in the moonless and stormy night. Even if we did make it to the village, we didn't speak more than a few words of Turkish. How would the residents react to our late-night request for help? Perhaps the most distressing bit of news: no one knew where we were, and we didn't have a phone. We had no way to reach the outside world thanks to our desire for an "off the grid" experience.

The night hadn't started that way. We arrived at our scenic camp spot shortly before sunset after a full day of walking along Turkey's famed Lycian Way. Fellow walkers touted this route to us as one of the most beautiful in the world, and it was living up to the hype. The azure blue of the Mediterranean Sea sparkled as we hiked along the rugged cliffs, enjoying the occasional respite from the heat in the pine forest areas. The packs we carried were 30 pounds each, loaded down with a tent and gear to go the full distance of 300 miles over the next few weeks. We'd planned this trip for months, and it was turning out even better than we hoped.

Earlier that afternoon we enjoyed a meal with two university students we met while walking. These first-time backpackers from the bustling city of Ankara chose to rent a room at a pension for the night. Warren teased them for carrying tents they didn't plan to ever use during their weeklong hike.

After goodbyes all around, we walked down the hill toward the sea, looking for a flat area to camp. As we rounded one of the hairpin turns on the rocky trail, we spotted a flat circular area surrounded by rocks overlooking the sea. It was beautiful. Our perfect little spot was just big enough for a tent and gave us a front-row seat to the setting sun over the Mediterranean.

It didn't take us long to set up our tent, change out of our sweaty walking clothes, and ease our feet out of our boots and into our flip-flops. We high-fived each other for scoring such a great location, feeling a little bit sorry for the university students we left in the pension. Were they going to see a magnificent sunset over the Mediterranean? No way. And they were paying for a night in a cramped room while we were sitting in the lap of Mother Nature for free. *Suckers.*

We perched ourselves on a boulder with our legs swinging off the side of the cliff, eating our bread, cheese, and olives for dinner. Our night's lodging was the best we'd ever had, anywhere in the world, and we knew it. As the sun set, we talked about our hike, our life, and the grand adventures we'd have before it was over. Little did we know the adventure would escalate that night.

At 1:30 in the morning, we began discussing our situation, neither one wanting to express just how scared we were. It was like two strangers making small talk about the weather in an elevator. *Can you believe this storm? Yeah, crazy isn't it?*

"I think we should pack up our bags now on the off chance the storm gets worse and we need to leave in a hurry," I said. Part of me wanted to hear Warren call me a worrywart and reassure me that I was overreacting as usual. Instead he agreed, reaching down to the foot of his sleeping bag to get his backpack. We took turns packing, since the tight confines of the tent didn't allow us enough elbow room to do it at the same time. While focusing on the task at hand, we spoke quietly, as if there was someone sleeping next door. I'm not sure why.

"We should sleep in our clothes, just in case we need to get up in a hurry," Warren said. We changed into what we planned to wear the next day and placed our rain jackets on top of our backpacks at the foot of our sleeping bags. The walls of the tent bowed in from the wind and the rain was pouring down, but we were optimistic that we'd ride out the storm. Against all odds, we fell asleep again.

At 3:20 a.m., I woke to a gentle caress on my cheek. I opened my eyes to discover the wall of the tent pushing down on my face. The wind was raging, and the aluminum poles in our tent bent at an unnatural angle. The rain pelted our tent so hard I thought it was going to break through the fabric. Lightning flashed over the sea, casting an eerie light in the tent every few seconds. The face we each saw in that greenish light was scared to death. It was well past time to pack up and get the hell out. But where? And how?

The storm in 2013 was a perfect parallel to where our marriage was just eight years before. Back then we couldn't even navigate our way through a regular weekday in the US together, much less a violent storm on the edge of a cliff in Turkey. Our relationship was on the brink of breakup. At first we tried to ignore the dark clouds gathering over our relationship. But over time the storm grew too large to ignore, just like this storm in Turkey. We could either find a way to safety together or let the storm destroy the relationship we built.

We chose safety.

We chose togetherness.

We chose to make our marriage work, and this is the story of how we did it.

2

Court Order

Warren walked up from the inner hallway in his faded blue jeans and brown leather boots. He stopped in front of where I was sitting in the reception area, cocking his head to the side.

"Who are you?" he asked.

I blinked at his abrupt delivery. He did have gorgeous blue eyes, and despite his blunt greeting there was a smile on his face.

"My name is Betsy. Who are you?" I decided to be as blunt as he was.

Instead of answering, he smiled again and asked me what I was doing there. I told him I was interviewing for a job, and he immediately took a step back when I told him the interviewer's name.

He said, "Whoa. Good luck; I think you're going to need it." There was a twinkle in his eye.

I shot back, "Well, he hasn't met me yet." It was lame, but the best I could do under his intense gaze. This guy was throwing me off my usual calm and cool demeanor, and I wasn't sure how to handle myself. It was 2002, and I was just entering my second year of the single life, moving from a small town in New Mexico to the Washington, DC area after my divorce.

Warren laughed, pointed his finger at me, and said, "I like you." Then he walked away. I still didn't know his name, what role he had in the company, or if he even worked for the company. It was possible he was just roaming from office to office raiding the break rooms for stale donuts.

I looked over at the receptionist and before I could say a word she just shrugged and said, "That's Warren."

After meeting the man who interviewed me, it was obvious Warren had been teasing. It was a relief to get the job, even though it was far from a dream position as a part-time consultant. But I had screwed myself up by leaving a good job early for a better one that didn't come through. I was scrounging in the couch cushions for gas money after a month without a paycheck.

My apartment was about 30 miles from the office, so in the beginning I worked from home and only came to the building for meetings. The first time I did, I was surprised to discover my desk was right next to Warren's. Due to the expansion of the company, the owners rented an entire new suite in the building and we were two of the first employees located in this sea of empty gray cubicles.

Warren spent most of his time away from the office, so we didn't see each other often. But over the next six months we became friendly due to the growing number of people near our age who began filling up those empty cubicles. The company was growing, and I was soon hired as a full-time employee. Our group ate lunch together and enjoyed after-work movies, bowling, and happy hours. Even though I liked Warren, he still had a talent for annoying me. He made funny comments about my dating life, using my search for love as a comedy routine to entertain our coworkers. He even left me obnoxious sticky notes on my computer with phrases like, "your boyfriend doesn't really love you." He was like a brother you liked but couldn't stand to be around for long. I began keeping details to myself, not willing to be the subject of Warren's Monday morning comedy routine.

One thing I admired about this cocky guy was his confidence and his laser-sharp observations about life. He was right about that boyfriend, even though I wouldn't give him the satisfaction of knowing it. He had a fearlessness I wanted for myself, and a comfort with saying what needed to be said, no matter what the cost. I considered him a bull in a china shop – someone to admire as long as you weren't breakable.

His position at the company was not an enviable one. He owned the task of turning around failing investments. He was the guy who had to make the unpopular decisions and was always on someone's shit list. But he seemed okay with it. I admired his ability to separate his ego from the blowback that often came from his unconventional solutions. He was only interested in results, and he got them. I was jealous of his ability to ignore popular opinion in the face of bigger, long-term goals.

I didn't know it at the time, but Warren was

reevaluating his first impressions of me, too. He liked it that I spoke my mind about work and life in general and didn't let anyone push me around – including him. He later said he fell in love with me over a debate about whether society benefits more from the existence of a god or the belief in the existence of a god. It was not the stuff of hot romance. My thoughtful and nuanced opinion on these types of issues contrasted with his black and white view of the world. This intrigued him.

It was the travel that clinched it for him, and what he thought it represented. I had recently returned from my first international trip, touring Italy and the south of France for two weeks with a friend. It was a cheap package trip in the shoulder season that I couldn't afford, but I did it anyway. (This was part of the reason I was so relieved to get the job soon after.) I didn't know at the time that Warren spent a life-changing summer in Italy during college.

Over the months we saw each other more frequently at work and after-hours social events with other coworkers. I began trusting him for honest feedback and advice on my work and how I should handle difficult clients. He had a knack for looking at problems from a long-term view and offered solutions that made my job easier. As a somewhat on-the-fly type of person (see: trip to Italy I couldn't afford), this appealed to me.

Warren began questioning me about some of my personal attitudes and how I was making a go at the single life in a new city by myself. He lived in a structured and rigid way, and he found my open attitude toward change appealing. We met at a time of dramatic upheaval in my life. I moved 2000 miles away from my small hometown after a divorce to make a new life for myself at the age of 30. Almost everything was new to me, and I was in a constant state of learning, adjusting, and moving forward. Looking back, I'm not sure he would have found me as interesting at any other time in my life. Either way, we each had a skill set the other one admired.

Our growing trust and respect for each other blossomed after a blunt conversation one winter morning. I had broken up with my first serious boyfriend since my divorce and moved closer to the office over the summer. Warren had separated from his wife earlier that fall and moved to another division a three-hour drive away. We were both in a state of transition, though his was fresher than mine. I was having lunch in the break room when he came to town for a meeting, and the usual crowd of people was gone. For once, it was just the two of us.

"Why do you think it didn't work out between you and your boyfriend?" he asked. He was contemplating his own future more than mine, and probably regretting leaving those sticky notes with the snarky messages on my desk. Even a breakup you want is still painful. I wouldn't usually answer such a personal question, especially to someone with the ability to push emotional buttons like Warren. But that day seemed different. He seemed to be looking for answers more than ammunition. I was seeing the softer, more vulnerable side of him for the first time.

I sighed and told him it was a partnership problem. I didn't want a husband, and I wasn't interested in being a wife. I wanted an equal partner to share my life, and my last boyfriend wasn't willing to go that far. I kept meeting men on opposite ends of the spectrum. They were either willing to let me pick up the tab and make all the decisions or on a mission to tamp down any independent streak they spotted. Where was the middle ground? I began to wonder if I was looking for the impossible.

Warren gave me that same wry smile he used the day we first met, and I felt a noticeable shift in mood. As I looked across the laminate table, it dawned on me that I was looking at the man in the middle of that spectrum, the one I'd been searching for all along.

We began dating long-distance, taking turns making the drive up and down I-90 from New Jersey to Maryland on weekends. I joked that he had to be toll-worthy to win my attention for the weekend, knowing I had to pay $12 each way plus gas to see him. Friday nights were always a long drive for one of us, taking at least three hours to make the journey. And the traveler often stayed until the wee hours of Monday morning before making the long drive back to arrive in time for work. We wanted to spend as much time together as possible. We never dreamed there would be a day we'd want to be apart.

When Warren's assignment finished in New Jersey he moved back to Maryland and into my apartment. We never talked about it in a permanent sense, and it didn't feel serious because he put most of his belongings in storage. We thought of it more like he was staying with me until he decided what to do next about work. After all, he wasn't a fan of my location in what I liked to call the "pre-gentrified" area of Silver Spring, Maryland. Yes, the guy across the hall from me sold marijuana, but he was also quiet about it and never had loud parties. I considered him a good neighbor. And yes, we once saw a woman throwing her boyfriend's belongings from the 5th floor out into the courtyard once. Two 10-year-old boys on bikes had seen it all before: "Oh yeah, she's throwing his ass out again!" Warren was not amused.

But the breaking point for Warren was after a night at the refurbished art deco movie theater in the downtown area. We saw an original print of *Cabaret* and stayed after the film for a Q&A with the actor Joel Grey. It was a classy kind of night, and I was hoping it would sway Warren's opinion of my developing neighborhood. While walking home and discussing the event, we came across a group of guys asking a friend to join them at a party. He leaned against the light post and took a long drag on his cigarette, blowing the smoke into the sky. "Nah, I gotta be in by 10 – court order." For months afterward, Warren emphasized everything he had to do with the phrase "court order."

It shouldn't have surprised me when Warren took me for a drive a few days later and showed me a house he'd found. It was in the suburbs, where no one loitered in the streets and the odds of seeing someone's clothes thrown out on the lawn were almost nil. I wasn't sure I wanted to live in the suburbs and said so, but Warren was definitely sure he didn't want to live in the city. In our first big compromise, we moved in together. Warren bought the house and assumed the financial risk and I moved away from the city and assumed the lifestyle risk. While I did agree to pay my part of the mortgage, I still can't believe he agreed to that arrangement, knowing I could bolt at any moment. From day one, he's been sure of our happy ending.

Three days before our wedding we went to the courthouse to get our marriage license, planning to return to the same place to get married. The courthouse in Rockville, Maryland is not the most romantic location, but since this was a second marriage for both of us we were more practical than in our younger days. Instead of the big dress and fancy party, we opted for a romantic honeymoon in Paris. We couldn't have both on our budget, so we chose the one that would give us the best memories.

Our path to engagement was relatively smooth. The daily actions of living together showed Warren that I wasn't going anywhere and he gave me the space and time to feel comfortable with the legal commitment. It was a win for both of us, the commitment-phobe and the serial monogamist. After about six months, we opted to move forward with marriage because of the public commitment, the tax benefits, and the legal rights it bestowed.

I worked mostly from home at my new job. After a long search Warren accepted a new job right down the street from our house that was to start the week after our honeymoon. Life was lining up nicely, and we couldn't wait to get on with our happily ever after. The hard part of getting to know each other and moving in together was behind us, or so we thought, and we were ready to enjoy the good life.

Warren's new company called the day before our wedding with a change of plan. "We've decided to move your position to our corporate headquarters near Boston. Are you still interested?"

Just like that, every careful plan we made went out the window. Warren looked for a long time to find this job, months of emailing resumes and interviewing. His savings was dwindling, and I didn't make enough money to cover all of our joint expenses. We didn't want to let the opportunity go, but we weren't sure about moving and starting all over again. Would it be too much stress for our new marriage to handle? Would his new job mean a pay cut for me if I couldn't transfer or find an equal job? We were in a quandary. We had just 24 hours to make the decision before getting married and leaving for Paris. The clock was ticking.

I checked the internal job listings at my company. Did we even have an office near Boston where I could work? There was nothing in my division, but there were several jobs listed, a few that would be promotions. I wasn't sure if I was ready to give up my current position, even if I stayed at the same company. Then we looked at the real estate market in our area. Homes were selling like hot cakes and for top dollar, so we were sitting in a sweet spot. But all that went away when you looked at the high prices in the Boston area. Any money we made off this house would quickly be put into another house, one probably more expensive.

With every option we checked, it seemed like a plus in one column and a minus in the other. There was no clear-cut winner, so we'd have to make our decision based on gut. What did we really want? I had to admit I wasn't crazy about where we lived. It was okay, but I was willing to trade in okay for the possibility of better. Warren was excited by the prospect of a great job, especially one with so much potential for advancement. And he lived in Boston once before, so he already knew he'd like it.

We joked about having a coin toss to decide, but in the end we each felt the pull of change more than the comfort of the status quo. He took the job. The night before our wedding ceremony we hardly slept a wink, thinking about the trip, the upcoming move, and the change happening in our lives. Were we making a mistake...pushing our luck, even? Or was this the smartest move we'd ever made? We'd soon find out one way or another.

The next morning we drove to the courthouse, me in my white linen pants and Warren in his button-down blue shirt. When it came our turn to get married, we entered the Wedding Room, where a sign by the door read, "Please do not throw rice." We stood in front of the lectern and repeated our vows to the clerk, feeling the weight of the moment even in the drab surroundings. We were getting married! For so long we looked on it as simply a legality to confirm what we were already doing. But the reality of the moment made us realize it was our first public statement of love. We were saying to the world, and to ourselves, that we were in this thing for good. I shivered at the thought and Warren reached over to hug me. He was feeling it, too. At the end, the clerk pronounced us married and we kissed, imagining the outlawed rice falling all around us.

3

Don't Hit the Snooze Button on a Wake-Up Call

We didn't arrive together, and we wouldn't be leaving together, either. When our work travel schedules overlapped in the same airport for just a couple of hours, we seized on the idea to meet for dinner. It was 2006, two years into our marriage, and we were yuppies through and through. How cool to have a date 2000 miles from home. We told everyone about it, reinforcing the image of our upwardly mobile love affair.

Warren was the casual corporate American male, circa 2005: khaki pants, a button-down, long-sleeved blue shirt, and leather shoes. He completed the look with impeccable personal grooming: clean-shaven face, recently trimmed thick, dark hair, and wire-rimmed glasses. Warren was Brooks Brothers handsome, a man on his way up. He'd been focused since he was a kid, idolizing Alex P. Keaton from *Family Ties* and dreaming about college and career when most kids are thinking about what they'll do on the weekend. His sock ties and drive to excel did not endear him to the other kids at school, but in adulthood it put him on the fast track to success.

My flat-ironed auburn hair shone from a recent trip to the salon, and my pale manicured nails and freshly applied lipstick completed the look. I was put together but not too flashy, competently attractive in a casual suit and scarf. I worked hard to lose most of the twang of my modest upbringing in a small town in New Mexico, speaking in a slightly melodic but strong voice. My image was carefully constructed to show my boss, employees and clients I had it together. I wasn't some small town girl who didn't know anything. *You can trust me*, it said. *I've got it under control.* I felt like I was always working to prove myself, the small town fish who'd awkwardly leapt to a bigger pond.

We were ambitious in distinct ways, Warren going after what he'd always wanted, and me justifying what I'd already achieved. This shared enthusiasm for our careers and the external rewards of traditional life first drew us together, and over time it outshone even our love for each other. We lived to work and achieve. Nothing else existed to define us, and while that sounds incredibly sad right now, at the time it just seemed normal. All of our friends – the ones we didn't have time to see – were the same way. "We should get together soon" became the standard goodbye in our circle of acquaintances and friends. No one meant it, least of all us.

As we settled into our table near the gates, parking our trolley bags to the side, we took in our surroundings. The televisions on the walls were tuned to the low buzz of the 24-hour news cycle, and the only live chatter we heard was quiet and one-sided: weary travelers calling home to people who missed them. The service was what you'd expect in an airport: staff who aren't concerned about repeat business because patrons are just passing through. No smiles, no friendly chat, just a bored stare with pen poised over the pad waiting for our order – not unlike the current state of our relationship.

A brief exchange with the sullen waitress resulted in two glasses of red wine and a plate of cheese and bread. We toasted and sipped, then quickly segued into a conversation about work as we picked at our food. We spent so much time wrapped up in our own lives that we were uncomfortable and out of practice in talking about our life together. The sexy date we imagined in a location 2000 miles away from our home outside of Boston vanished when it slammed into the boring and stiff reality of our relationship.

It was an awkward dinner, and those people we were so interested in impressing would have probably pegged us as coworkers instead of lovers if they were watching. This date was barely warm, much less hot. The silence wasn't comfortable, and the conversation was stiff. We both glanced at our phones to see how much time we had left before we could tactfully exit and go to our gates. I wanted to get back to reading my book, and Warren wanted to catch up on email. After being apart for several days because of travel for work, we should have been ravenous for each other, and instead we couldn't wait to get away again, especially if we could tell people how devoted we were to each other to meet up in Denver like this. If only they knew.

The past two years had been a slow downward spiral in our relationship. After the move to Massachusetts for Warren's new job, we began drifting apart as we dove into our careers. We were tied to our email, our laptops, and the maintenance of the house we bought in the Boston suburbs. Our attention was tuned to everything but our relationship. Our marriage was dying from neglect, even though we lived in the same house and shared the same bed.

I grew up in the desert Southwest, where storms can be sudden and vicious. The sky turns a strange shade of green right before the hail starts to pelt the ground and wind whips up into a tornado. Lightning flashes all around. Being caught out in a storm like this can be deadly, so people are attuned to the changing sky in the late summer afternoons. But sometimes a storm is obvious in approach, or even predicted by the local weatherman on the nightly news. You have time to prepare, to batten down the hatches and seek shelter.

Our relationship was like this slowly approaching storm, only we weren't paying attention. And the more we ignored the small drops of rain and increasing wind, the closer we were getting to the damaging hail and deadly lightning. That night in Denver was the dawning of that realization for us after a year of ignoring the warnings. There were no audible alarms and certainly no commitments to change. But this night at the airport did reveal the level we had allowed our relationship to sink to as we pursued our individual goals and dreams. We were dashing off in different directions, on that night and every other night, and if we didn't do something about it soon we'd arrive at separate destinations, never to be reunited.

We split the bill for our dinner, each tucking a receipt into our bags for work expense reports. We hugged tight, knowing there was a shift happening in our relationship but unwilling to voice it. Finally, Warren released me and said, "Let's talk on Saturday, okay?"

Such a casual statement, but loaded with so much meaning. I nodded my head and blinked back a tear as we turned to walk away from each other yet again.

4

A Concrete Life Raft

Back in the tent in Turkey, as the storm raged around us, that scene from eight years prior in the Denver airport was like watching a movie. How had we ever been those people? We felt as disconnected to our past selves as we once did with each other.

After packing our things and dressing in the next day's clothes, I awoke to the wall of the tent pushing down on my face. It was past time to leave. We quickly began packing up our sleeping bags, which were already covered in sand, and calmly talking through our next steps so we'd be on the same page. It would take both of us working together to get off the cliff without losing our tent – or worse.

The backpacks stayed on the floor of the tent to weigh it down against the wind. We took our hiking poles from the vestibule and laid them inside the tent so we wouldn't trip over them or leave them behind. We'd need them to get up the hill. The headlamps were strapped to our heads and cinched tight before we turned them on. We put on our rain jackets, and then took turns lacing up our shoes and stepping outside the tent.

This peaceful camp spot had turned into a wind tunnel. The rain was falling up, down and sideways, with the large boulders around us acting to harness and force the wind down and around our tent. Rain slapped against our faces, dozens of tiny needle stings every second. The wind covered the sound of the sea, but we could see the white caps of the churning waves even in the darkness.

Our next moves reminded me of every film that's ever been made where the hero has to do the impossible, like get through a room of laser beams or scale a 100-story building, to escape the bad guys or find the treasure. I tried not to think about the mishap that always occurs in the middle of these challenges to increase the risk for the hero. We had enough drama at the moment.

The scene was a choreographed dance of removing the stakes to the tent flysheet right after a gust of wind and quickly running together toward each other in the dark to mash it between our bodies and keep it from catching in the next gust of wind and flying out to sea. We walked sideways, pressing the flysheet between us chest-to-chest, to the laundry bag we had weighted down with a rock, and shoved it inside. Then we threw the bag inside the tent and zipped the door shut. Next we began dismantling the tent underneath, pulling out the bent poles and packing them in the sack. Because Warren had put rocks on the individual stakes the first time we woke up, it was easier to find them and pull them from the ground. I appreciated his forward thinking as we stumbled around in the dark to dismantle the tent.

I stood on the back of the flattened tent to hold it down as Warren pulled our backpacks and poles out, and we quickly stuffed the tent and ground cover into the laundry bag and strapped it to the back of Warren's backpack. The time for folding and properly packing the tent was a long way off. We hefted our backpacks up, surprised at how easily these 30-pound packs caught in the wind and pushed us against the rocks and precariously close to the edge of the cliff. I thought about the weight we'd lost over the past few years and silently wished for about 20 pounds to return to help hold us down. Armed with our poles to keep us steady and our headlamps at full beam, we began the slow and careful trudge back up to the village in the pouring rain.

The good news? We had gone this way before, so it wasn't completely unfamiliar. The bad news? It was still a slick, rocky path on the edge of a cliff and the wind was heavy enough to make us feel like paper dolls in front of an electric fan. Random thoughts came into my head, like wishing I had kept with Pilates so I would have stronger core muscles to keep me upright and wondering what my mom was doing at that exact moment.

Every minute or so we called out to each other, making sure we were both okay in the dark. Our headlamps barely made a dent in the darkness and heavy rain, and we could hardly see the next step in front of us. It was a fine balance of staying close enough to not get separated but far enough apart that one of us falling wouldn't also knock the other one down. While neither one of us wanted to get hurt, we knew if it happened the other would need to be strong to get us out of this bind. It was a weird combination of a "fend for yourself" but "stay strong for the team" mentality.

We finally made it to the main dirt road that led to the village of Alinça and breathed a sigh of relief. The storm was still raging, but being off the slick rocks and away from the edge of the cliff meant we were at least out of danger of being swept out to sea. This was the longest and most dangerous mile we'd ever walked. We trudged on, trying to remember the few buildings we'd passed the day before and hoping to find shelter.

The first building we came to was a vacant-looking pension with a covered porch, our life raft in the storm. We climbed up the steps as quickly as our heavy packs and the wind would allow, free from the pelting rain for the first time since we left our tent. This shelter was out of the storm, dry from the rain, and partially protected from the wind. Despite still being outside, we finally felt safe.

The backpacks were quickly dropped and we took off our wet shoes. We settled in against the wall on the hard concrete floor right next to an open door. We hoped it wasn't filled with stray animals, but we figured they'd probably be smart enough to stay inside and away from the storm. It was now after 4 a.m., and without any options, we huddled together under a sleeping bag for warmth, leaning against each other in exhaustion. The sky flashed with lightning over the Mediterranean Sea as we finally dozed off in our concrete bed.

We awoke at daylight to a man standing in front

of us smiling. He pointed to the open door of the room we'd slept next to and then pantomimed sleeping by laying his head on his hands. We looked around the corner and saw it wasn't a vacant room at all, but a fully made up room for guests. There were even towels folded at the end of the bed.

The man was the owner of the pension and lived nearby. He made a habit of leaving the room open for nighttime visitors who might come along after he'd gone home. He stopped by every morning to see who had stayed and to cook breakfast and collect payment for the night, knowing most visitors would be walkers like us.

We laughed at ourselves for not realizing a bed was available to us all along, and we gladly took him up on the offer of Turkish breakfast: eggs, cucumbers, olives, tomatoes, cheese, and bread. We were giddy at having escaped our dangerous situation. The rain was still falling and the wind still blowing, but we were safe, dry, and fed. We weathered the storm together, working as a team, and we made it through to the other side. We felt like we could face anything together, and experience proved us right again and again.

5

The List That Changed Everything

When we got married in 2004, we bought a perfect house in a perfect neighborhood and had two perfect jobs...or so it seemed. But the winds of reality soon started blowing and we saw the downside to this vision of perfection.

The commutes were awful, and we spent more time in our cars than we did with each other. I drove 45 minutes south down I-495 to get to work near the border of Rhode Island, and Warren took the opposite commute north toward Boston. The effort of staying on top of our jobs and managing a house and yard too big for our needs meant our relationship fell to a very distant third priority. Actually, it was more like fourth, because we lavished our dog Max and our cat Roo with the love and attention we denied to each other.

The work travel schedules were brutal, and we often went days without seeing each other. We spent a lot of time silently blaming each other for why this wasn't working out.

As it got worse, we buried our heads in the sand and worked harder, blamed more, and wondered why the other person just couldn't get it together. The phrase *"Do I have to do everything myself?"* played in a continual loop in our heads until we'd convinced ourselves we were each single-handedly keeping our relationship together.

After one particularly bad fight about lying and secrets and flirting with other people, every topic except the real problem of not being committed to each other, I stormed out into the night. I didn't really trust Warren after discovering some flirtatious emails. He assured me they were harmless and he had no intention of following through, but I was gone as much as he was for work. Who would be the wiser if he had an affair? He could even be sleeping with other people in our own bed. The more I thought about it, the madder I got.

Maybe I should have an affair. That would show him. I thought about it as I drove, listing candidates in my mind. *He wasn't the only one who could still attract attention.* I drove until I knew he'd be asleep and then quietly returned home, sleeping in the guest room for the night. The next morning was an uneasy truce as we did our usual dance of trying to make things look right while ignoring the nitty-gritty of the problem. As long as we could cover it up, we were okay. We drank our coffee and left for work, going in opposite directions as usual.

But it wasn't so easy to keep a storm quiet. The more I thought about him having sex with someone else, or even just wanting to, the less I wanted to have sex with him. So I pulled away physically, even denying him everyday contact. It was a regular complaint of his from the very beginning of our relationship, my ability to build walls and hide myself from him. In fact, it's probably what made the flirtation so appealing to him in the first place. Instead of coming together to resolve our problems, we each retreated to our own defenses. We were fighting about nonexistent affairs when our only infidelity was in our commitment to each other. But it was easier to focus on the possibility of people on the outside than it was to look inside our own marriage.

We finally went to a therapist to see if he could fix us. The office was in an old building on Main Street, and we both left work early to make the appointment. That showed commitment, right? Neither one of us knew what to expect. This marriage therapist had the look of a distracted genius, sitting behind a large desk full of papers, envelopes, and books. With his gray and black beard, slightly too long hair, and wire-rimmed glasses, he reminded us more of a college professor than a therapist. We settled onto mismatched chairs among the stacks of books on the floor and then we just stared at him, neither one of us knowing what to say. Was this a test? Were we passing or failing? As always, we were concerned with how we looked from the outside.

He smiled and finally asked us why we were there, and we hemmed and hawed. The answer required honesty, and we weren't quite ready to go that far. To say it out loud would make it true. To dodge the bullet of full disclosure, we sugarcoated our problems and softened the strength of our feelings. Ironically, we came together to downplay the severity of our disconnect, acting as if we'd almost stumbled into his office by accident while out shopping. He must have known we were hiding our problems, as we can't have been the first couple to do it. But we thought we were so smart, checking off the "see a marriage therapist" box in the accepted list of "how to fix your relationship" actions. How long did we have to see him before we could say we'd really tried?

We found our escape by ganging up on the therapist after each session. "He talks too much," we'd say. "Do you think he's even married himself?" we'd ask. "I don't think he can help us," we'd agree. After just two sessions, we called it quits, blaming him for not being able to cure us when we withheld every important piece of information from him and from each other.

As time went by, we mostly ignored the growing distance. Work consumed us, as did fixing up our house, and we spent our time making sure our relationship looked good from the outside. If that were true, then the inside would surely fix itself.

I got a promotion. Warren got a raise. We had the outside of the house painted from sunny yellow and blue to a more somber gray with black shutters and a red door. The yard was landscaped. This work on the exterior of our lives was the solution to the interior problems. Or so we thought.

It wasn't until we met at the Denver International Airport that we realized things were at rock bottom. If we could only make time together in an airport 2000 miles away from home, our priorities were out of whack. It was time to acknowledge the elephant in the room and make a decision one way or another.

Are we in this together? *Really* in this? If so, we knew we had to start acting like it.

As I waited for Warren to return home from his business trip after our date at the Denver airport, I thought about the start of our relationship, how we drifted together, and the sparks that flew once we collided. It was electric back then, and now we couldn't even muster the equivalent of a burst of static electricity from walking in socks across carpet. I knew Warren was thinking the same thing: What in the hell happened? Where did that bright hot blinding love, lust, and joy go, that willingness to move together toward adventure and the unknown? Were we finally realizing the impact of opposites attracting and changing into something else?

Those hot, sexy people who leaped into this opportunity together were not the same drab, boring couple who currently occupied their house, performed their jobs, and sometimes couldn't stand to be in the same room together.

How did we get so far apart? Was there a path back, and did we even want to make that journey? Those were all questions for our reunion, and we weren't sure how it was going to play out.

The Saturday morning after the Denver airport dinner we brewed a pot of coffee and sat down across from each other at the kitchen table.

"What is it you really want?" Warren asked.

It was easier for me to tell him what I didn't want: the long commute, the big house, a life in the lonely suburbs, the lack of control over my work schedule and inability to have a social life. The lack of friends even if we did have time for a social life. The lack of connection with him and the doubts about our commitment to each other. The lack of passion and feeling of being unwanted and overlooked. The lack of even a variety of food choices in our small bedroom community. I think he was shocked at the list of negatives that came out of my mouth. So was I.

The relief of saying it all out loud caused me to realize the enormity of our problems. I felt a lack in every area of my life, both with him and without him. But saying it out loud also gave me an insight I didn't have before. And at that moment, I realized most of it was of my own making. Every single thing I listed could be changed. It was a flash of insight, a glimpse into a different future, and it both thrilled and terrified me.

My grandmother used to say, "The devil you know is better than the one you don't." She was my primary caretaker as a kid while my mom worked at the Levi factory to pay the rent. Granny smoked like a chimney, lived like a hermit, and saw the world through a filter of fear. She oozed judgment toward people who didn't play by her rules, and her rules were simple. Don't change. Don't rock the boat. Don't take any risks. For years she ridiculed my mom, calling her "Miss Astor," as in New York socialite Brooke Astor, because she dreamed of a better life. Granny couldn't understand why mom worked at the Levi factory when she could sit home and make almost as much in government benefits as a single mother. Mom was caught between needing her and resenting her. The difference in the two women was obvious even to a little kid like me. Granny had a certain level of comfort as long as she didn't challenge her fear. Mom had no comfort as she left her difficult childhood and moved forward into the unknown on her search for something better. Both women were in a box, but only one of them wanted out.

Granny was a complex woman, and since she never talked about her upbringing I don't know what made her so afraid of change. But for years I wanted to be the anti-Granny. She was my motivation not to be stuck, miserable, unhappy, and powerless. Even as a teenager I could see how she was walling herself in, only allowing people near her if she could control them completely. I vowed I would never do that. The image of my grandmother flashed in my head as Warren and I had the conversation. If I stuck with the devil I knew, would I turn into her? The thought made me shudder.

I turned the question around to Warren, "What is it you want, and does it include me?" I held my breath waiting for his answer.

Warren focused not on what was lacking in his life, but what he wanted to add to it. He has always maintained that regret is a wasted emotion and he wanted no part of it. What happened was done, and instead of bemoaning it or wondering, "what if," the only logical solution was to move forward. In the beginning of our relationship, I thought this was a load of self-deluding bullshit, but since we all have some level of bullshit we want to believe about ourselves, I let it pass unchallenged. Who didn't have some regret in life? But over time I realized he was serious about this. He didn't look back at all, sometimes to his detriment.

A drunk driver killed Warren's father when he was 10 years old. That night Warren was at home, watching television with his 8-year-old brother. The phone rang and his mother answered, never expecting that her life was about to turn upside down. Her husband Rick had been in a horrible car accident, and he wasn't expected to survive. She quickly bundled up Warren and his brother, already in their pajamas, and took them to a neighbor's house. Early the next morning, she was there when they woke up and told them their father was gone.

Warren remembered the last weekend he spent with his father on a Boy Scout camping trip. It was the only time he'd ever had his dad all to himself, and he'd never experience that again. Over the years, he missed all the usual father-son rituals: playing ball, fixing things together, having the awkward sex talk, sharing a beer while watching a baseball game, introducing girlfriends, and planning college and career. And while most men would regret that, he instead looked at what he had because of his loss: a closer relationship with his mother, a strong drive to succeed quickly and enjoy the fruits of his labor, and a no-BS way of looking at life. He shed tears over the loss of his father, but he also knew he'd be a different man had his father lived. And he liked the man he had become.

It's hard to argue with that logic, even though it seems harsh. So instead of focusing on what had gone wrong in our relationship and life, Warren characteristically looking forward at how to adjust and make it better – with me. He wanted a shorter commute, since the notorious Boston traffic was one of his biggest stress triggers. He wanted to walk more, to have a neighborhood with people like us, and plenty of restaurants to choose from. He wanted to become a known regular, a part of the community. He wanted sushi and Indian food and Thai food and time in our schedules to eat them at a leisurely pace with good conversation. He wanted dates with me on a regular basis and nights out with friends. He wanted more time at home on weekends and evenings. He wanted to have more sex.

I sighed in relief. We were saying the same things, just from different ends of the spectrum. A closer inspection would have revealed that we often did this.

We took out a piece of paper and began making a list. Now that we had identified the problems, how could we fix them? We knew what was contributing to this storm of unhappiness, and now we needed to find a way to bring ourselves to safer ground. We focused entirely on our environment and what we could change to have less stress and more time together. As it turns out, this was quite a lot.

After we made this list of major irritants, we started brainstorming the ways we could reduce or eliminate them.

The idea we came up with – to work on achieving what we wanted first instead of trying to fit what we wanted into what we already had – was revolutionary for our relationship. It freed us up from the blame game and those negative feelings of oppression from environments, responsibilities, and relationships we didn't like and gave us permission to pursue the environments, responsibilities and relationships we wanted in our lives. We stopped thinking about how to shrink less and looked to expand more.

First we listed all the things in our lives we'd like to change:

Long commutes in opposite directions

Heavy travel schedules for work

A house with too much maintenance and upkeep to manage

A location too far from the social life we wanted

The requirement to drive everywhere

The inability to plan any social events due to rapidly changing work schedules

Too much stuff to feel free

The last remaining bit of credit card debt

Then we listed all the things we'd like to have in our lives, and we used specifics:

Less than 15 minutes of commute time

The ability to walk to at least 9 different ethnic restaurants from our front door

A smaller house by at least half with half as many belongings

Zero credit card debt

A social event at least every week

A work schedule that left evenings and weekends open

A neighborhood with a mixture of homes, restaurants, shops, and green spaces

After we had our lists, we began thinking of all the ways we could make this happen. We didn't censor ourselves at this stage and let every single crazy idea come up. After all, we didn't have to commit to them just because we said them out loud.

Talk started with moving, possibly even living in another country. How hard would that be? What about changing careers altogether? Could we fix up old houses and sell them? Maybe we'd manage property for other people, or open a bed and breakfast. What about our more creative colleagues who were starting tech and service businesses? Maybe we should invest our time and money in someone else's great idea. The options were endless, and the more we talked it out, verbally exploring every idea, the more we honed in on what felt good to us both.

Eventually we realized we'd both have to change jobs to knock out a lot of negatives and add in some of our positives. My job only required that I live near an airport, and I was pretty certain I could get at least a lateral transfer in the company to a job with less travel. My hope was to find a better job within the company like I did when we moved to Boston. Warren knew his job would need to change entirely, and instead of looking in the Boston area, where prices were high and jobs were harder to find at the time, we decided he would look elsewhere.

In the past, the first course of action in job-hunting was to spruce up the resume and start looking for what fit. This time, we decided to consider our list of lifestyle goals and match them to cities that had the kind of jobs Warren was qualified for and at a cost of living we could afford. We vowed only to look for jobs in places that fit our lifestyle requirements. Three cities made the cut: London, San Francisco, and Seattle.

We quickly ruled out London and San Francisco because the tech job market for both areas was outside the city proper. After living in the suburbs twice already, we knew it wasn't a good fit for us. That left Seattle, and Warren focused his efforts there. It wasn't too long before a company came calling, one located right off Puget Sound and in the heart of the city.

He flew out for the interview right after we called a real estate agent to discuss the options for putting our house on the market. The interview went well, and while we were awaiting word we decided to list our home. Whether he got the job or not, we knew we'd have to move to have the kind of lifestyle we wanted.

We spent our second anniversary in Kennebunkport, Maine, away from our laptops and our jobs. It was a good start to rebuilding our relationship, and we were excited about the plans we had for recapturing our love and our lives. A few weeks before I would not have laid a bet on us making it to anniversary number three, but at that point the confidence was returning. Warren got the call while on the drive back home from our weekend away. In just one month he'd be starting his new job 3,000 miles away in Seattle.

The timeframe from making our list to the day we moved to Seattle was only two months. It's hard to believe we made such sweeping changes in such a short time. Once we started moving on what we wanted, it all seemed to flow. We got caught up in it, and the momentum carried us forward.

That list saved us. It jump-started our failing relationship and allowed us to start dreaming of a future together again.

6

The Revelation from Intoxication

When the phone rang and I heard my dad's voice on the other end, I knew something was drastically wrong. My dad doesn't know anyone's phone number, even his own, and he won't use a smart phone or even an answering machine. Mom was always the one who called and later handed the phone to him. I don't know that my dad had ever called me before in my life. My gut clenched.

"What is wrong with mom?" I asked, holding my breath. Oh please, oh please, oh please don't let anything happen to Mom. My heart pounded.

"Calm down, honey. Your mom is okay. I'm calling to tell you that Bo has had a heart attack, and he's on his way to the hospital in Lubbock. We're on our way there now." Dad's voice was even, but I could tell from 2000 miles away he was working hard to control his anguish over my brother. I wasn't as strong, and I dropped to my knees and cried out so deeply from my gut that I didn't recognize the sound was coming from me.

It was 2007 and we were enjoying our first year of living in Seattle. We patted ourselves on the back pretty often over the transition we made in our lives after that date in the Denver airport and our subsequent life-changing list. Life was good, and we felt like we had the world by the tail. It was an illusion of control that shattered when I got that phone call from Dad.

The day was normal. I went to a business meeting at a restaurant for lunch, and afterward I was in my kitchen, looking outside at the tree in the alley and admiring the spring blossoms. It was time to take the dog for a walk, and then I had a couple of phone meetings scheduled. It was a typical workday up until Dad's phone call.

I don't remember calling Warren at work to tell him about it. I don't remember him coming home and making flight arrangements or packing my bag for me. I don't remember the drive to the airport to catch the red-eye to Texas. What sticks in my mind most is the realization that my hard-working brother who had everything to live for could be dead before I even arrived. I was numb at the realization that life doesn't always work out as planned. At the same time I was worrying about my brother, my subconscious was saying, "Hey, if this could happen to him, it could happen to anyone, including you."

Warren stayed behind in Seattle, ready to pack more clothes, kennel the dog, and fly out later if need be. My youngest brother Jeff picked me up at the Lubbock airport the next morning, and by his welcoming smile I knew Bo was still alive. We went directly to the hospital from the airport, bypassing coffee, breakfast, and even a chance to brush my teeth after an overnight flight.

Seeing my brother in the hospital bed in a ward full of old people shocked me. Bo has always been bigger than me, ever since we were toddlers, so I've only nominally been the "older" sister. But he looked so small on the bed, and the grayish cast to his skin was the first clue that he was far from well. This was not supposed to happen to a 35-year-old man. He worked hard, played by the rules, and then something completely out of the blue changed his whole life.

As I watched him improve over the course of the week, Warren and I had long conversations in the evenings via phone. What did this mean? How could this happen? Was it genetic? We didn't have any answers, only questions. When Bo was out of the biggest danger, those thoughts in my subconscious began rising to the surface. *This could happen to us.* After all the time spent re-imagining our lives, moving cross-country and changing jobs, we felt in control of our destiny. Bo's heart attack reminded us we weren't. Anything could happen at any time to blow all our plans to smithereens.

On one hand this thought was freeing, and on another it was terrifying.

Warren and I were shocked at Bo's heart attack and what it said about the fragility of life at any age, and we knew we were going to make some big changes. But as Bo got stronger and the medications began improving his condition, we began dialing back our worries about him and about our own lives. We drifted back to our former lifestyles with only a few words here and there about chasing dreams and living up to our fullest potential. We slowly sank back into the comfort we had with our life, ignoring the urgency for change we felt while Bo was in the hospital until it just wasn't urgent anymore.

This was all standard human behavior, of course. We wanted to explain the tragedy to create distance from it. The more distant it felt (as in "time heals all wounds"), the less we identified it with our current selves. And the less we identified it with our current selves, the less pain we felt and the less it impacted our current lives.

So we kept explaining why what happened to Bo: a) wouldn't happen to him again, and b) would never happen to us. We were safe and could go back to our normal lives, all of us. We reasoned ourselves right back into complacency, as if we were in control.

Talking ourselves out of crisis when it was no longer immediate was shockingly easy to do. Life went on as usual for about a year, until we were again reminded that a well-planned life is not immune to outside forces.

Paul and Maria were two good friends we made in Seattle. Maria had long, curly red hair and an expressive face. She was vivacious and outgoing. Paul was more serious, a stoic Scotsman with a dry sense of humor. The two of them made a lively pair, and we enjoyed their company very much. They were a lot like us, only a few years younger: 30s professionals with a dog, no kids, and living in a townhouse. Maria and I were both in the business of working with women entrepreneurs, and Warren and Paul both worked at the same tech company and rode a work shuttle together every morning. Paul and Maria were part of the reason we felt so at home in Seattle. Because of people like them, we didn't feel out of place like we had in the suburbs of Massachusetts.

Maria and Paul were both family-oriented people, and they were shocked when my brother had his heart attack. Over the months afterward, they continued asking about him. We even had a few of those "life is short" conversations while drinking wine and feeling pretty insulated from the outside world.

A year after Bo's heart attack Maria suffered a brain aneurysm at home, falling into unconsciousness in the bathroom. Though he rarely did this, Paul was working at home that day and heard her fall. His quick call to the ambulance got her to the hospital in time to save her life. But what kind of life was it going to be? She was in and out of consciousness, blind in both eyes, and her signature mane of curly hair was shaved off to insert a shunt to regulate the pressure still building in her head. She went from being a ball of energy running a thriving business to a tiny, bald shell of a woman who couldn't remember what she'd just said or even sometimes who she was talking to. She spent weeks in the hospital recovering, though none of us knew how far she'd get.

We were worried about Paul, who was trying to hold down a job, take care of his wife, and manage their finances without her income. He didn't know how far she would recover and what quality of life they would have together. Warren and I began having discussions with each other about what we'd do in the same scenario. How would we react to a similar circumstance in our mid-30s and beyond? There was no real way to plan for an emotional and financial toll like that, especially out of the blue. All those feelings and memories from Bo's heart attack came flooding back, and we winced a little at not learning this lesson the first time someone we loved got blindsided by life. There was no backtracking this time, no talking us back into complacency. Just like the date at the Denver International Airport, we were standing at a crossroads and knew we had to make a change in direction.

Our conversations began to shift to the one thing we did have some control over: how to live as full lives as possible for as long as possible. We started talking again about that list of what we wanted in our lives.

A few weeks into Maria's recovery, while she was still in the hospital hoping to regain her strength, eyesight, and short-term memory, we spent a holiday weekend evening at a local Mexican food restaurant with two good friends. All four of us knew Paul and Maria, and naturally we discussed the situation. What would become of them? If the same thing happened in our own relationships, what would become of us? This was a normal extension of worry about someone we knew and loved – someone very much in our same age/occupation/social sphere – who was hit by tragedy.

As the night wore on and margaritas were consumed, we became more daring in our conversation. "What ifs" took over, and we let loose in ways we wouldn't have without the lubrication of alcohol or the knowledge that our friend had such an uncertain future.

Warren asked around the table, "What would you change about your life right now if you knew you wouldn't make it to 40?"

That was the question that changed everything for us. As we went around the table answering, Warren and I locked eyes, both thinking of our long-term dream of retiring and traveling the world. If we wouldn't make it to retirement age, could we travel now? It seemed strange to contemplate at the relatively young age of 37, but as we let the idea sit with us it grew more comfortable. And soon it felt exactly right.

Why couldn't we travel the world before retirement? We could save up some money, rent out our house for a year, and either take sabbaticals or quit our jobs and find new ones when we returned. We didn't really have anything tying us down, and we had already paid off our credit card debt as part of our big lifestyle change when we moved to Seattle. We were each ticking off these details in our minds as we looked at each other, our logical brains working in sync because we had been so focused over the last couple of years on streamlining our lives to make room for what was most important: our relationship. We had already downsized our lives, moved cross-country, and created the lifestyle we wanted. Why couldn't we go a step further and travel the world for a year?

"We'd travel the world!"

It was out of my mouth before I knew it, and Warren was nodding his head. Our friends readily agreed, in the way you do when an idea sounds fun but you have no real plan of making it happen. But we knew it was different for us. The air was electric between us, and it was the first time we'd ever felt so connected, as if we were each thinking the exact same thought, riding on the same brain wave, our hearts beating in tune.

The next morning I woke up to find the other side of the bed empty. I lay there for a while thinking about the night before and all that was said and unsaid. Butterflies churned in my stomach and I didn't know if it was the revenge of the margaritas or the idea of traveling the world that we unleashed the night before. Probably a little of both.

I walked downstairs and found Warren at the kitchen table, coffee on his left and his laptop open in front of him. I asked him first if he remembered what we'd discussed the night before, and he looked up and smiled.

"I'm already researching how we can travel around the world."

I poured a cup of coffee, sat down next to him, and we began planning our grand adventure.

7

Out with the Old

Two years. That's how long it took to uproot our lives and finance a trip around the world. During that time we stayed focused on our goal and gradually stripped our lives and budget of everything that didn't work toward our dream. We saved money like never before, got rid of everything we owned, and eventually gave up habits we knew we wouldn't take on the road with us, like cable television and microwavable food.

What started as a plan for a one-year trip around the world with a sabbatical morphed into an open-ended journey with nothing to tie us down. The dream just kept getting bigger, so our existing life had to get smaller.

Along the way we learned a few things about each other. More accurately, we began to deeply experience things we already knew, and it wasn't always easy. For instance, Warren is gung-ho and loves the start of anything. *Anything*. He's excited and wants to do it all at once. He's the kid who started packing for college the day after high school graduation, even though he had three months to wait. It was not so different with this trip. Within a week of making this decision, we knew we had to get rid of some of our stuff. To rent the house out meant putting our things in storage, and we didn't want to pay to store things we didn't really need. So he began Craigslisting at least one item per week, usually more. Selling our unwanted stuff through this online classified ad website became a game for him, a way to actively work toward our goal while we were doing more passive things like saving money and researching destinations.

Our previous experience using Craigslist was always for a specific reason: an upcoming move. This was different because we had such a long time before our departure and no real way to know how much we needed to get rid of. From my perspective, he was rushing things. I didn't want to start living without anything right away (it was still two years away, for heaven's sake!), and it was a bigger leap for me to imagine what life was going to look like in the future. I wanted the comfort of my things and the status quo while I slowly imagined myself morphing into the future. The more he pushed to sell, organize, plan, and save, the more I felt like things were being taken away from me. Warren felt like I was not committed to the plan and forcing him to be in charge our motivation. He thought this was unfair.

This is another indication of our differences, in that Warren is hot and cold, and I'm a slow burn. It takes me a while to get mad or excited, and it frustrates me when he gets gung-ho as much as it frustrates him when I don't jump with enthusiasm at every idea. This was something we already knew about each other, but over the course of our time preparing for the journey we got to know it in excruciating detail.

Warren wanted to sell everything right away. I had to warm to the idea and eventually had a Reverse Birthday Party, letting my friends "shop" through my favorite possessions on my last birthday before leaving. I needed to get used to the idea over time and have friends to help me through, along with plenty of wine and good food. Warren indulged me, and the result was a spectacular party with many new memories to replace the old possessions. But without Warren's gung-ho attitude we would have never cleared out an entire house in time. We're a little like Goldilocks and the Three Bears: he's too fast, I'm too slow, and together we're just right.

Despite these differences in style, there was no doubt we were becoming a stronger team. Over time, we began appreciating our differences a bit more and how they could be merged to make a stronger team. One way this worked was in trying new things. It made sense as our life was being emptied of possessions and responsibilities to add in some new experiences. Our big trip was going to be one big adventure, so why not practice a bit before leaving? The more we did these new things together or supported each other's individual pursuits, the closer we felt to each other and to our trip. By working together toward a bigger dream, we were more in sync in our smaller daily goals, too.

I trained from a couch potato start to run in a half marathon the summer before we left on our journey. I was overweight by 50 pounds and hadn't run since childhood, so it was probably not the most logical pursuit. I followed the "Couch to 5K®" training program online, finally working my way up to 5 kilometers (about 3 miles) of running without walking.

It was a relief after starting at just 60 seconds of running, and I was surprised at how quickly my body adjusted and improved. Then I switched over to the training program for the half marathon, which starts at being able to run 5K. A good friend ran with me most mornings.

One day near the end of our training she was out of town and I had to do an 8-mile run by myself. I was feeling a little cocky as I dressed that morning in my running gear. I was about to run farther than I ever had before, and before even setting out I knew I could do it. There was still a lot of junk in my trunk, but I knew how to move it. With my ear buds in place and Storm Large singing *Ladylike*, I started jogging down the sidewalk. The most intimidating part of my run was through the University of Washington campus, where lots of students ran much faster than me. As I left the campus and headed toward home, I ran along the path to Lake Union. I neared an apartment building wrapped in scaffolding and heard some yelling. It was good-natured, so I turned my iPod down a bit so I could hear. The feminist in me wanted to ignore the catcalls from the construction workers, but the fitness freak in me wanted to be acknowledged for clocking the time to make my body healthier (and hotter).

As I was having this internal debate, the yelling got louder. I sucked in my gut, pulled back my shoulders, and tried to look my strongest as I ran past the building. That's when I noticed there weren't any construction workers. I stopped running and turned around just in time to see a Duck Boat drive past, the goofy tour leader telling jokes about Seattle and encouraging all the tourists on board to make noise and blow into their kazoos. They didn't even notice me! I broke down laughing at myself, sitting on the curb as I wiped the tears from my eyes. Just when I began taking myself too seriously, life brought me back to normal. I put my earbuds back in and resumed the jog home, gut on display and smile on my face.

Later that summer when I ran the Seattle Rock 'n' Roll Half Marathon, Warren was at the finish line cheering me on. The roar of the crowd was far more satisfying than the fake catcalls from my training run, and the hug from him at the end sealed my victory. Afterward we gorged on hamburgers and beer with friends and he took funny pictures of me soaking my feet in an ice bath. I haven't run since.

Sometimes we tried new things together. After a lifelong fascination wondering if blondes really did have more fun, we bleached our hair. Our house was sold and we were renting a couple of rooms from a friend for our last summer in Seattle. She was out of town for the July 4th weekend and we were feeling adventurous. Why not bleach our hair? Worst-case scenario, we were leaving the country in a couple of months and no one would have to see it. We walked to the neighborhood drugstore and searched the shelves for the right color. How blonde did we want to go? We finally settled on L'Oreal™ Feria 205 Extra Bleach Blonde.

Back at our friend's house, we stood in the bathtub and took turns painting the bleach on each other's hair. The goo from the kit didn't allow us to see much of what was going on underneath, and we couldn't decide if it was working or not. We sat on the edge of the bathtub while the timer on our laptop ticked away.

At 25 minutes, Warren bent his head over the tub while I washed out the bleach. I wrapped his head in a towel so he couldn't see it yet. Then he washed my bleach out and wrapped my hair in a towel. We turned and faced the bathroom mirror together and on the count of three we whipped off our towels to reveal what we hoped were white-blonde locks of cool-looking hair.

Ta-da! Looking back at us in the mirror were two orange-blonde people. We laughed at the difference, especially with our dark eyebrows.

We dried our hair and took pictures to post on Facebook, not realizing the camouflage effect of our orangey hair in a room with yellow walls. At the time Warren wore his hair in almost a buzz cut, so his grew out in just a few weeks. I kept buying packages of bleach every 10 days or so. I was determined to get that white-blonde look, and I thought the bleach was no more harmful than the hair dye I used for years – until my hair started breaking off. I just wanted to shave it all off and start over. Two weeks before we left on our trip we stood in the bathtub together again while Warren shaved my head with the same clippers he used for his. It was an intimate experience, trusting him to shave my head, and one Warren claimed was just about the sexiest thing we'd ever done together. Reconnecting to celebrate or commiserate after trying something new together was pretty strong glue for our partnership.

We became more comfortable with looking silly, making mistakes, and going after not-so-normal things, like Warren's final adventure before we left on our trip.

Just a few days after moving into our new townhouse back in 2006, we were exposed to an annual event in our neighborhood known as The Solstice Parade. At the summer solstice every year, there was a parade like no other. There were no live animals, motorized vehicles, printed words, advertisements, or logos allowed in this parade. Everything was human-powered and handmade, and the results were a hodgepodge of moveable art, dancing, and clever social commentary.

As part of the appreciation for Mother Nature, there was always a swarm of naked bicyclists who crashed the start of the parade, most with elaborate body paint of animals, plants, or even superheroes. It was the least sexual nudity we'd ever seen, and it fit perfectly with the tree-hugging vibe of the parade.

Still, questions swirled in our minds: "How did they comfortably ride a bicycle with no clothes?" and "Who painted these people?" and most of all, "Why were they naked?" There was the hot silver guy on the skateboard, the parents with their daughter in a wagon decorated as a patch of strawberries, and plenty of elaborately painted cats and wild animals. It was incredible to see such a blatant display of innocent and fun-loving nudity (dare we say "family friendly" nudity?). In fact, that first year Warren said the words that would come back to haunt him, "I'm going to ride in this parade next year!"

He didn't, nor did he do it for the next three years. The parade came around one more time the final summer we lived there in 2010. After years of saying he was going to ride naked on his bicycle and backing out, Warren got the support of our good friend Katy to do it with him. Her now-wife Karen and I were the "body painters" of our respective mates, and we spent a good couple of hours up close and personal as we painted them in a mutual friend's basement. Warren wanted to be a globe, and I put a blue coat of paint all over him before adding continents. Our friend Katy wanted her body tie-dyed. Karen and I finished painting them about 30 minutes before the start of the parade. Since the bicyclists aren't a sanctioned part of the parade, they have to crash it, racing to the front to signal the start of the parade to the thousands of people watching from the sidewalks.

Since it was Seattle, there was of course a bit of rain. We opened the garage door and Warren and Katy mounted their bikes, naked except for their helmets and shoes, and wished them well.

Warren looked back at me and said, "I don't think I can do this."

Knowing he needed a bit of tough love, and remembering that I just painstakingly put blue paint in places I should never see up close in the clear light of day, I told him he couldn't back out and quickly closed the garage door. He was naked outside, and he knew I wouldn't let him back in until the parade was over. Karen and I washed our hands of paint and walked down to the parade.

Warren and Katy sped down the hill on their bikes, racing through the major intersection in front of the drawbridge that connected to the Fremont neighborhood. And then the lights went on. Boats were passing below, so the drawbridge went up. Because it was so close to the start of the race, car traffic had already been stopped and there were only pedestrians on the bridge – hundreds of them. Warren sat on his bike, mortified, because he and Katy were the only naked people on the bridge. Everyone was going to the parade and knew about the naked cyclists, but there was safety in numbers. And right then, the number of naked bicyclists was only two. Warren kept his eyes straight ahead as he waited for the bridge to open. A kid nearby said, "Mom, that's Africa on that man's leg!" He could barely breathe his anxiety was so high.

Once the bridge lifted Warren and Katy rode like the wind to the start and then enjoyed the attention of the crowd who loved their bravery and creativity. His insecurity melted away among the fun-loving crowd and other body-painted bicyclists. At the end of the parade route, he and Katy put on some clothes and met us at our favorite burger joint. We laughed about their nervousness and cheered their bravery as we drank beer in the sunshine. Warren complained, "of course there is no rain now that I have clothes on."

Later, we wrote about it on our website, showing a strategically posed picture of Warren in his blue body paint. A reader who was at the parade and remembered the "globe man" found the photos she'd taken and emailed them to us. Our joke became that he was the only man on the planet who received naked pictures of himself from women he didn't know.

He ended up helping this same woman get an interview at Microsoft before he left, and a few years later we met her and her husband in Amsterdam for dinner as they were traveling through. Though of course at the time we never realized Warren being naked in a parade would lead to a new friendship.

With all of our new experiences during that time, we didn't realize we were planting the seeds of much good fortune and friendship in the future. We were simply following our dreams, large and small, and saying yes to new opportunities even when they scared us a little bit.

When our date of departure arrived, we had done a lot of weird stuff together and separately, including branding ourselves with tattoos, taking trapeze lessons at a circus, and Warren jumping out of an airplane. We were not adrenaline junkies by nature, but the feeling of freedom we had after getting rid of all our possessions made all these activities seem absolutely normal. We didn't say no to anything even remotely interesting to us, and we suddenly had time for all those things we never got around to before. This sense of adventure in our everyday life brought us closer together than ever before, and it prepared us for the incredible journey ahead.

8

You've Got To Be Kidding Us

Quito, Ecuador (CNN) — *Ecuador's
government appeared teetering on the verge of
collapse Thursday, as national police took to the
streets of Quito, the capital, and physically
attacked the president over what police said was
the cancellation of bonuses and promotions.* ~
CNN.com

Just another hotbed of political activity in a faraway
country, right? Except this was actively in progress on
October 1, 2010, the day we were finally leaving on our
long-awaited trip around the world. First destination:
Quito, Ecuador.

Everything was in place after two years of careful
planning and work. We had scrimped and saved, sold
our house and all our belongings, and spent the
summer saying goodbye to our friends and family.
Our only agenda item for the day was to get on the

plane at 11:55 p.m., meeting the deadline we set 25 months before with just 5 minutes to spare.

Warren saw the news first. "The airport in Quito is closed. It's a coup," he said.

I looked up, not understanding what he meant. "What do you mean, *coup*?" He read the article out loud to me as I sat with coffee cup half raised to my lips, staring in disbelief. The president was holed up in a hospital where he'd gone for treatment of injuries sustained in a tear gas attack. The National Police surrounded the hospital and wouldn't let him leave, and they stormed parliament as well. From the hospital the president declared a national state of emergency, and the military were out in force to bring the situation under control. The army was trying to bring the National Police in line. Guys with guns trying to restore order from guys with guns – this did not sound good at all.

Tires were burning in the streets, the national highway was blockaded, and the country's two main airports in Quito and Guayaquil were closed. Protesters rallied outside the hospital and policemen tear-gassed the crowd. Behind the scenes, the government and National Police were wrestling for control of the national television station, with employees chaining the doors so the police couldn't enter.

Live video feeds showed the mayhem online. We looked at each other, wondering what to do. Our house was sold, our possessions were gone, and we'd quit our jobs. We had one-way tickets to Quito. We had a place to stay in Ecuador for the next few weeks and a friend of a friend coming to pick us up at the airport. Were we going to blow our carefully constructed budget on day one of our journey with expensive, last-minute tickets somewhere else? Or was this a sign we weren't quite ready for this lifestyle?

A coup d'état was something that happened in scary, unstable countries, not the equatorial paradise where we were headed. (If we'd done our research we would have known this was a not-too-uncommon occurrence in South America.) It was hard not to go into freak-out mode, watching our plans unravel after 25 months of planning and preparation.

But then the light bulb went off in our heads. We were seeking adventure and an up close lesson in cultures around the world, and we'd just stepped into history in the making. We smiled at each other, jumping to the next revelation in this line of thinking: we had absolutely nowhere to be. If we wanted to, we could change our trip entirely at that moment. We could go to Asia, Australia, or even Europe. We could go to another South American country. We could even road-trip our way down to Mexico from Seattle.

This was the dawning of what our new normal was going to be, flexibly swaying to whatever held our interest or adapting to current political or weather fluctuations. For the first time in our lives, we were free to go and do what we wanted without timelines or restrictions. If we wanted to fly into an attempted coup, we could do it as soon as the airport reopened. We could divert to neighboring Bogota, Colombia. We could do just about anything.

Warren called the airline, whose phone agents were unaware of the situation in Ecuador. The agent said they would not fly into a closed airport or a hostile situation, and since we had a long layover in Miami why not just wait until arriving to make a final decision?

We couldn't imagine purposefully "waiting out" a political situation while casually eating Cuban food in Miami. What kind of people were we turning into? It was frightening and exhilarating.

Day one of our adventure reinforced a lesson we learned when we first started creating the plan to turn this dream into reality, and that was to keep moving even when we didn't know the answers. Action forced the questions to be answered in a way that analysis did not. I don't know why we sometimes forget this lesson because it has proven true again and again in our lives. And this time was no different.

Warren, the planner of our relationship, was uncomfortable with the idea that we were going into this without an itinerary (something we laugh at years later because we never have an itinerary anymore). I was a nervous Nellie because my over thinking brain was worried about everything. It didn't help that I had started taking altitude sickness pills the prescribed 24 hours in advance and they were making me jumpy and tingly. Despite all this, we pushed forward and stepped into the somewhat unknown.

That night we bid a teary farewell to our friends and then we went to our gate, ready to fly to Miami. This adventure was not starting out as we expected, and we wondered how well we were going to adapt to this lack of structure and stability in our lives. Leaving everything we knew meant no one was going to help us make these on-the-fly decisions. We were on our own, and we had to depend on each other completely.

Even though we knew this logically going in, it was far more real sitting at the airport with all our worldly possessions in just two backpacks. This was the first of many "I knew this was going to happen but not like that" kind of feelings.

In Miami, we walked out into the hot air and waited for our friend Pat. We had seven hours before our flight to Quito – if it actually happened – and we planned to enjoy a Cuban lunch with her while we waited.

We still weren't sure where we'd be sleeping the following night. Our decision was made and we were going forward, but almost all of it was out of our control. It was a weird feeling, almost freeing because it absolved us of the worry of working it out. We simply had to go with the flow, adapt to the situation, and keep adapting. As people who were used to trying to control and plan everything (didn't we just spend two years doing this?), it was uncomfortable. We had enthusiasm on our side because of the thrill of the adventure ahead, but we were still working through the issues internally. Warren wanted to plan it out and know the details. I kept thinking of all the unknowns and worrying about how we'd adapt once we got there. We didn't even speak the language.

As we returned to the airport, full from mojitos and fried food, we laid odds on whether or not the flight was going to happen. As we approached our gate, we saw the sign lit up with our destination: Quito, Ecuador. On Time. This "leaning in" bit was a lot easier while we were still in the U.S.; getting on the plane was another thing altogether. But we did it, trusting that if nothing else the fear of lawsuits would prevent a major airline from flying United States citizens into harm's way.

Four hours was all it took to transport us from the life we knew to the uncertain future ahead. It was so mundane on the airplane – *would you like nuts with your soda?* — but inside it felt a roller coaster. We sat quietly in our seats while our brains and guts started a riot. When we arrived at the Quito airport, the dichotomy continued. The immigration officer stamped us into the country as if he was almost asleep, but there were uniformed men with guns all over the airport. We didn't know if this was normal or in reaction to the coup attempt.

Gustavo met us outside holding a sign with our names on it, and we were relieved to have a local contact to help us weave through this mess. Or at least that's what we thought. When we looked out the windows of Gustavo's car, the mess didn't seem so bad. There were a few tires burning on the side of the road as we drove through, but no blockades. People were out walking in the streets, and had we not known there'd been a coup attempt, it wouldn't have registered as anything other than an average Saturday night. Our stomachs started to unclench and we enjoyed the quiet conversation in the dark car as we rode through the mountains, away from the big city.

We arrived at the house at midnight, a cozy rammed-earth cottage overlooking a valley where we could just make out a few lights in the ranch house below. The backpacks were quickly dropped, and we pulled off our clothes and snuggled under the heavy wool blankets in the cool house. The mental and physical exhaustion of the past 24 hours caught up with us.

We could barely remember the disconnected, bored, and loveless people we were just a few short years ago when we had our big wake-up call at the Denver International Airport. Those people wouldn't have made it through the last 24 hours together, much less the 25 months we spent planning for this grand adventure. No, those people weren't as strong or vulnerable as we were, and we were glad to have left them behind.

That night, we settled in for the deepest sleep of our lives.

9

Parasites and Passion

Warren's eyes were circled in black, even though he'd slept for 10 hours straight. His skin was pale, and he was exhausted despite the sleep. He barely ate, and he was losing weight fast from chronic diarrhea. We were just two weeks into our dream journey, and my husband was falling apart. The first few days I blamed it on our newly healthy diet and the altitude. We'd gone from eating mostly happy hour food at sea level at the goodbye parties in Seattle to a mostly vegetarian organic diet high in the Andes Mountains. Surely we'd acclimate to the altitude and fiber intake soon.

Every morning at the ecolodge, we'd arrive for breakfast in the dining room. Our house was a private home on the property and not officially part of the lodge, but we treated ourselves to breakfast there every morning and cooked in our kitchen for our other meals. It was a great way to practice our Spanish, and the food was delicious.

The head of the kitchen was an indigenous woman named Petra. She wore the traditional dress of the native Quechua people, a crisp white blouse with multicolored embroidered flowers and a long dark skirt. Her glossy black hair was tied back in a colorful ribbon, and she wore woven sandals on her feet. Petra may have looked like she stepped out of the past, but she had a good laugh over our fascination with foods her people had been eating daily for a thousand years. Every morning there was something new and unusual, and every morning we went through the same question and answer routine in our broken Spanish.

"*Qué es eso?*" What is that?

"*Desayuno.*" Breakfast.

Petra would smile before elaborating on the unusual fruits and dishes in front of us. *Tomates de arboles* – tree tomatoes – were blended to make a tangy juice that soon became my favorite breakfast drink. *Guyabano*, a spiky tropical fruit, was another delightful discovery. On the table every morning was a dish of garlic, onion, and peppers called *ají*. Ají was like ketchup to the Ecuadorians and they ate it on everything from soup to meat to eggs and potatoes. We had plantain dumplings, savory steamed corn *humitas*, and breakfast soups made with hominy. There was always bread, mostly made from the yucca plant, and homemade cheese along with blocks of brown sugar called *canela* for sweetening. The ecolodge had a garden out back, so every meal also came with greens, and our tea was made from fresh herbs steeping in the pot, also a new thing for us.

When Warren asked Petra how something was made, she responded with a sly smile and a phrase like "love" or "magic." He wasn't getting any recipes from her. She smiled every time, poured him more coffee, and gave him extra portions with every meal. Warren adored her, and she set the tone for the kind of warm and funny interactions we'd seek with other locals around the world, especially over food.

Even with Petra's delicious cooking, Warren was losing weight and feeling worse. Petra sent over special tea in the afternoons to help settle his stomach. The taste was bitter and awful, but Warren drank it anyway. I watched my healthy and energetic husband lying listlessly on the couch, barely eating after breakfast and gulping water to stay hydrated. I began worrying that he was regretting our decision to travel. What else could it be? We were in paradise and eating the healthiest food we'd had in years, or perhaps ever. He must be stressed or worried about something.

I knew of a scientific theory called Occam's Razor, which stated that the simplest answer was probably the right one. I resisted this line of thinking because my brain worked in a convoluted way. Simple didn't last long in the dark alleys of my mind. Why go with the easiest answer when there were hundreds of other solutions that were more interesting?

Like many overthinkers, I prided myself on my ability to see between the lines and intuit feelings and motivations other people couldn't see. I just *knew*. And in this case, I knew Warren was pushing something down and making himself sick. I considered it my job to figure out what was wrong. The more he resisted my questions, the more convoluted my thinking became. Warren's illness had to be psychosomatic, a physical manifestation of the angst of leaving his career and traditional life behind. As his partner, I was bound to help him get over it...even if he didn't think he had anything to get over. In fact, *especially* because he didn't think he had anything to get over.

Losing traction in a career had always been a bigger concern for Warren than it was for me, as his identity was far more tied up in his work. He was in the business side of the technology industry for 20 years, and he built up a nice career. Mine had also been good, but I left it a few years before to start a small consulting business, so I was already out of the career ladder mentality. I felt like I could come back and pick up freelance or consulting work anywhere, especially since our expenses were almost nonexistent. But Warren struggled with the thought of leaving his career, knowing the people who were his peers and below him would surpass him in pay grade and experience while he was traveling. We had several conversations about this during our planning phase, and at the time I wondered if he would later look on the trip as a bad move. Would he regret losing his place on the career ladder? Would he resent me for it?

Warren told his coworkers about our trip over a year before our departure, giving them plenty of time to get used to the idea. He pitched a specific job to his boss that took him out of his normal duties and worked on special projects for the remainder of his employment. This transitioning so early on paved the way for saying goodbye. Warren had over a year to gradually break away from corporate life. I worried telling his boss so soon would cause more stress and possibly cause him to lose his job, but he judged the situation correctly and used it to his and the company's advantage. Because we were so open in talking about it for months beforehand, and because Warren was proactive in the way he managed his departure, by the time I picked him up for his last day of work, he was done with the corporate life. Done with the career and the worries about advancement. Done with the cut-throat competition. Done with fighting uphill battles. Done with it all. He got into the car at 3:00 on the afternoon before our departure, and we drove off the Microsoft campus toward our future.

But here we were just a few weeks later, and I was rethinking that drive away from his job, wondering if his feelings were very different after cashing the last paycheck and saying goodbye to his seniority.

"Are you feeling sad about leaving your career?" I asked.

He said no, but did he really mean no? Or was he covering it up because he didn't want to disappoint me? Or because it was too late to get his job back? Maybe spending all his time with me was not as interesting as he thought it would be. My mind was working overtime on this question, and I knew I'd break him soon.

"Do you miss our friends?" I prodded.

"Of course I miss our friends. But I'm not sad. Would you just stop with this?" Warren's frustration with my questions should have been an indicator I was off track, but in the odd workings of my brain, it only cemented my suspicions. He was hiding something from me, and I was getting close.

In the meantime, Warren tried to rally. We walked through the giant market in nearby Otavalo, the largest open-air market in South America. The woven crafts were beautiful, and we bought fresh fruits and vegetables to cook at home. At night, we'd bundle up in heavy wool blankets and walk up the stairs to the flat roof of our casa, lying down to watch the explosion of stars in the inky-black sky. We learned what light pollution was and why we'd been blocked from seeing the actual night sky our entire lives because of man-made light. It was stunning.

Three llamas lived at our ecolodge. A baby llama was born just before our arrival, and the managers named him Rafe, after Ecuadorian President Rafael Correa. Each morning in the field next to our house, Rafe's mom would be loosely staked to the ground so she'd eat the grass in that area. Rafe would stay close by his mother, though occasionally he would venture into our yard out of curiosity. Rafe looked more like an overgrown stuffed animal toy than a living being. Warren spent a lot of time lying on the couch and looking at the llamas through the window. Occasionally Rafe would come up to the mud brick house and lick at the paint, which was actually a combination of salt and chalk. The minute we'd come to the window he'd run off, caught in the act like a petty criminal.

Life at the ecolodge house was bucolic. Llamas grazing out the door, long-tailed hummingbirds drawing nectar from the explosion of orange and pink blossoms surrounding our whitewashed house, and a stunning view of the snow-covered mountains from every window. We had fresh fruit and vegetables, warm blankets and a comfy bed, and a front-row seat to the show of stars every night. We even had Internet. The two lodge dogs slept on our porch every night, mainly because the homeowner left a stash of treats for us to feed them. It was an ideal spot.

So why was Warren so worried and making himself sick? I couldn't understand it, and I was starting to get mad that he wouldn't talk to me about it. I asked him repeatedly what was wrong, and he repeatedly told me he just didn't feel well. I wondered how long it would take for him to finally spill the beans.

One day I was talking to the manager of the lodge, a Frenchwoman named Catherine, about Warren's illness and how I just couldn't shake the feeling that something was really wrong. I focused on the mental and emotional changes we'd gone through, and she took a much more practical stance.

"What is he eating and drinking?" she asked.

I told her that besides breakfast at the lodge he wasn't eating much at all, just guzzling water to stay hydrated. And then I wondered why we were focusing on such basic questions when it was obviously something deeper and more mysterious.

"You mean he's drinking the tap water?" Her brows furrowed at the question.

"Of course he's drinking the tap water." I was starting to get an uneasy feeling.

"The tap water is not safe. There is no filter in that house, and if you want to drink it, it has to be boiled for 10 minutes first. You know you can come get filtered water from the lodge kitchen if you need it, right?"

The light was starting to dawn on me. Warren was actually sick from the water, not from any psychosomatic illness. I'd been pestering him for two weeks, worried he was battling some internal demons when in fact he was battling intestinal parasites. You'd think someone newly arrived in a country would first look to the food and drink as the culprit for illness, but in my overthinking way, I projected my fears and uncertainties about our lifestyle change on Warren. Instead of trying to make him better, I was trying to make myself better by analyzing this projection. It was *him*, not me.

The main reason I didn't think it was the water was because I didn't get sick. At the time I didn't drink a lot of plain water. I boiled mine to make tea or coffee or drank fruit juice from the filtered water in the lodge kitchen. Warren drank at least two liters of water straight from the tap every day, further poisoning himself every single time. When we told the homeowners about this problem, it turns out they were tea drinkers, too. They didn't have stomach problems because they boiled their water.

This was the first of my many attempts to overcomplicate our lives. Instead of taking what Warren said at face value, I projected every fear and worry I had into what he wasn't saying. I looked around at the llamas, hummingbirds, mountains, and stars and wondered why I felt so unsettled. This is what we wanted, right? Then why did I feel so scared?

We worked for two years to make this dream happen, and now one of us had intestinal parasites. The other one had an inability to take information at face value. I was seeking something other than what was already revealed, assuming a depth and meaning that wasn't there. I was looking for answers to my own insecurities and worries in other people instead of in myself. If I didn't get my overthinking under control and learn to appreciate what was right in front of me, this was going to be a very long and complicated journey.

One round of antibiotics later, we had at least one problem solved.

10

The End of Privacy

When we finally figured out the cause of Warren's illness, we started joking about how much we were learning about each other in this newfound togetherness. With one bathroom and absolute stillness on the top of the mountain, it was hard to hide when he was sick. And with a weight loss and continuing illness over weeks, we stopped being polite about those things. I needed to know if he was on the verge of dehydration because of the diarrhea, because I was the only one to find him a doctor and get him there.

In our life before, bathroom time was private time and the door was always shut. We didn't even pee in front of each other, and that was fine with me. I didn't want to see, hear, or smell his bodily functions, and he didn't want to become familiar with mine. Everything that fell under the category of personal hygiene – grooming, laundry, bodily functions – remained private and separate. I argued for years that it would take the romance out of our relationship to be exposed to our most basic functions.

And here we were, living in silence at the top of a mountain, sharing one bathroom, and navigating an adjustment to a diet of mostly vegetables and fruits with a few intestinal parasites thrown in for fun.

"Can you go outside for a while?" Warren would ask.

He wanted some privacy, and I obliged by sitting on the porch swing to read or walking with one of the lodge dogs. Warren could have his privacy, but to ask for it meant I knew what he was doing. It felt weird for both of us to announce our bodily needs this way.

My god, I thought. *Are we becoming hippies?* I wondered just how casual we were going to become with each other in this new lifestyle and whether we were ready for it. The thought of him scratching his balls or picking his nose in front of me made me want to gag. And clipping my toenails or plucking ingrown hairs in front of him would surely be the deathblow to any desire he had for me. Would we even be able to look each other in the eye after all that? I shuddered at the thought.

Despite my worries, over the next few weeks we became attuned to our bodily rhythms on top of the mountain and barely acknowledged out loud this giant leap forward in our comfort level with each other. We didn't reveal more than needed, but we stopped being squeamish about what was perfectly normal. What we knew about love and romance, at least our version of them, was shifting. Did this mean we were wrong before, or that we were making a mistake now? It's hard to step back from that level of intimacy once you're in it. Since we didn't have many options for privacy in the current situation, we just went with it.

My arguments about it ruining our romance didn't hold up over time. The more transparent we became, the closer we felt. It just became normal. We'd never be the types who keep the bathroom door open and the conversation flowing while taking care of our personal business, but we did learn to acknowledge it as part of our human existence without killing our sex drives.

This was certainly not the kind of story you'd find in a grocery store romance novel, but it was working for us.

Nothing was turning out exactly as planned, including our adjustment to the pace of this life. It was like getting married in a way. Even though it was a good thing, and we looked forward to it, there was still a great deal of stress at the changes. We loved the freedom and experiences of our new lifestyle, but adjusting to it was still, well, an adjustment.

Our relationship was changing just as fast. We built this dream together, working our separate roles to make it happen, but in the reality of it, we were now full and equal partners, that thing I always wanted. There was no one with a specific role of going to work, networking for clients, commuting, cooking the meals, doing the grocery shopping, paying the mortgage. Everything we knew as normal was gone, and even though we asked for it, we hadn't recognized the enormity of change we'd experience in this new life.

We went from spending a few hours together every day to spending every hour together every day. All those secret habits we used to do alone – snacking, watching porn, surfing online – now had to be done in front of each other or not at all. It was humbling and embarrassing. Sharing a laptop was perhaps the worst.

The auto fill feature on the URL led us to discover where the other person had been surfing, and it was sometimes surprising.

"Who is Perez Hilton?"

Ugh. I was embarrassed that Warren discovered my secret celebrity gossip addiction. At 40, I felt like I should have outgrown this about 20 years before. But still, I checked in with my pal Perez every day for juicy gossip and kept myself up to date on movies I'd never see, people I'd never meet, clothes I'd never wear. But it wasn't just me airing my secret habits.

"You might want to clear the cache next time," I'd warn him after discovering porn. He'd turn red from embarrassment, even though I didn't care that he looked at porn. I just didn't want to see the evidence of his solo activities when I was logging on to check my celebrity gossip. We had to air our most embarrassing habits in front of each other, those silly little rituals that had always been our personal escapes. Some of them we let go out of embarrassment (no more jumbo packs of Twizzlers™ to gnaw through while Warren was at work), and some we learned to embrace in a more open way, like setting up a folder for Warren's porn so I didn't have to see it.

The other change we didn't count on was the increased intimacy. It wasn't just the sex, which took on a new dimension as we adjusted to being completely on our own without responsibilities. (Yay for everyday vacation sex!) And it wasn't the increasing comfort with personal body habits, either. In one of the biggest leaps forward in our relationship, Warren finally learned something I'd been keeping from him since day one of our relationship.

We were at a race track on a sunny afternoon, learning how to place bets in Spanish. It was our first time to watch horse racing together. We walked to the racetrack, misjudging the start time and arriving very early. The stadium looked a little run-down, like a grand old place that had seen better days. If we squinted we could imagine people getting dressed up to come here in decades past, though the only people we saw that day were a few grizzly old men with racetrack papers gripped in their hands and cigarettes hanging from their lips. Since we were two of only a few people already there, and the only ones buying food and drink, the staff waited on us hand and foot. We sat at our table under an umbrella in the warm sunshine and sipped ice-cold beers as we waited for our food.

The groundskeeper was still working on the track, tamping down the dirt and spiffing up the winner's circle. We walked down to the railing to get the groundskeeper's attention and asked him if we could stand in the winner's circle. He shrugged as if it was okay, and we didn't wait for any further encouragement. We hopped over the railing and walked across the track to the winner's circle to take goofy pictures of ourselves.

Right next to the winner's circle was a scale with a huge digital readout. Jockeys weighed themselves and their saddles before and after every race to make sure there was no cheating with weight, in full sight of the audience. Since we'd both been losing weight with the healthier diet and daily walking, plus a bonus round of intestinal parasites, we were curious. How much had we lost?

Warren nudged me and asked if I wanted to step on. I shook my head vigorously. We might be cozy about bathroom time, but there was no way in hell I was going to weigh in front of him.

He hopped on first and the display lit up for everyone in the stadium to see. The readout was 67.6 kilograms. My eyes lit up at that, realizing it wouldn't show pounds. It was still hard to get used to metric measurements and Celsius temperature readings, but outside the US this was the norm. Maybe my weight wouldn't be so bad in kilograms.

I looked around, noting only a few people in the stands, and then stepped on the scale myself. I'd never disclosed my weight to any romantic partner before. And there I was stepping on the biggest scale I'd ever seen. The number flashed: 80.4 kilograms.

We high-fived each other and laughed at the idea of weighing ourselves at a racetrack because we didn't have access to any other kind of scale. But the biggest laugh of all was that we had no idea what those numbers translated to in pounds. We had to wait until we got back to our laptops to check the conversion and figure out how much weight we'd lost!

Knowing each other's weight, and supporting each other as we tried to get healthier, was one of the most intimate things we'd ever done. We didn't have to try to fool each other anymore with dark colors and body shapers. After all this time together, we were finally sharing exactly who we were, right down to the numbers.

PART II: WE'RE NOT IN KANSAS ANYMORE

11

The Aliens Have Landed

Drunken men leaned against the cement walls relieving themselves of excess beer, and children ran around the square squealing in excitement. Life-sized straw men were everywhere, in the shape of policemen, comic book villains, and old men. It was late in the evening on New Year's Eve in this small village near the border of Ecuador and Peru, and instead of fireworks we were going to witness actual fires. At midnight the crowd torched these effigies, called *"los viejos"* for old men, releasing the bad memories and experiences of the year and clearing the slate for good fortune to arrive. After three months of traveling and getting used to this new 24/7 lifestyle of togetherness into the unknown, we were excited to see what the new year would hold for us.

We didn't have an effigy of the previous year to burn, but if we did, it would have been a small one. After a lot of change in our lives, we were starting to feel as if it was the new constant. New experiences and situations didn't faze us as much as they did before, and we were taking more things in stride. Earlier that morning we'd gone for coffee and overheard a conversation – a serious one – about aliens and groupthink and a New Year's gathering of some conspiracy theorists in the area. Once upon a time that would have shocked us, but after so many new experiences in the previous few months, we began to expect the unusual. Our effigy probably should have been a little alien straw man, because that's how we often felt as we moved through this new world.

In the past three months, we'd stayed for two weeks in Baños, Ecuador, a town below an erupting volcano. We watched the rocks spew and the lava churn every night. The windows in our guesthouse rattled with every belch of Volcan Tungurahua, but we trusted the locals who said the eruption – if it even came – would go around the town, as it had in times past. Every day there was a fine coat of ash on everything. And every day we couldn't believe we were staying another night. What kind of daring souls had we turned into?

A trip to Colombia was cut shc t because of hundred-year flooding and roads being washed out. We tried to find a way through via plane, bus, and private car, but it just wouldn't work. We finally turned around, only to discover the border in Ecuador bottlenecked due to a computer outage. It was Christmas Eve, and a hundred people were in front of us waiting to get stamped into the country. We were stuck in the no-man's-land between Colombia and Ecuador and wondered if we'd have to bed down on the street for the night. Finally, we found a cab driver and asked if there was any way around this mess, strongly hinting we were up for just about anything at that point. He had a "cousin" in the immigration office, and for $20 he offered to get our passports stamped. In just 15 minutes, we were on the other side of the border and our first bribe.

There were hundreds of smaller examples of expanding our comfort zone and adding new skills. We learned how to bargain after growing up in a fixed-price society. In social settings, it became easier to distinguish between those trying to con us and those wanting to get to know us. And we were making progress on learning Spanish and being able to communicate better.

This feeling of being outsiders and newbies had a benefit, though. Our lessons in flexibility and leaning in to discomfort together made us feel confident to face just about anything together. We were learning that everything can be figured out, and moving forward with action was the best way to encourage those answers to materialize. While we had some challenges and problems in the previous year, they paled in comparison to the problems of the past because we were finally working together to solve them. This sounded so obvious in hindsight, but we simply didn't work that way before. It was always a battle over whose way was the right way, personal position over shared interest. Once we stopped trying to win arguments and instead looked for solutions in our common interest, the game changed completely. We were still fighting, of course, but this was the most productive fighting we'd ever done. And when it was over, it was really over.

We woke the next morning to a silent new year, most people relishing the day off and nursing hangovers from the night before. We made our way to the bus stop in the twilight, starting the first leg of a long journey to get to the isolated mountainous city of Chachapoyas, Peru, home of the ancient Cloud People.

We watched the landscape go by as we listened to the Spanish music through the tinny speakers on the bus. Tired looking women with babies strapped to their backs with a shawl were the most frequent passengers, along with their toddlers, and I wondered what their lives were like. Were these women older than me or younger? It was hard to tell. I wondered if they had any control over the size of their families. Most likely birth control was not an option here due to economic and religious reasons, and I couldn't help but feel grateful for the reproductive choice I'd had in my life. Birth control was always available to my sexual partners and me. Would these women choose differently if they could? Smaller families, longer spacing between children, or even no children at all? Or was I imposing my Western standards as superior when they were in fact just different?

In almost every interaction with a South American we were asked about our families. Where were our children? How many did we have? You could see the look of pity in their eyes when we told them we didn't have any. It surprised us because we don't feel sadness over this very conscious decision. A lightbulb finally went off when we realized we were doing the same thing to them, but in reverse. They pitied us our tiny little family of two, away from our extended families as we traveled. And we pitied their large and boisterous families in the face of so much poverty. Was our way superior? Were they happier? Hard to say either way. The more we learned about the world, the less sure we were of any hard and fast rules.

After a few hours we arrived at the Zumba bus station, which at that time was little more than a dirt parking lot and a few shacks. With stomachs grumbling, we pulled up plastic stools at one of the food carts and ordered a chicken and rice meal to tide us over. The day was hot and dusty, and we had to put out of our minds the worry that the chicken wasn't refrigerated or that the utensils weren't clean. So many of the things we worried about before now came with a different set of rules. The chicken wasn't refrigerated; it was killed that day and plucked for cooking right away. Eggs weren't refrigerated because they were used within hours or days of gathering. We had to keep reminding ourselves the old rules didn't apply, and that the people who lived there were doing just fine eating this way. Why couldn't we?

When a flat bed truck with wooden benches pulled up a couple of hours later, we boarded for the two-hour ride to the border of Peru. This kind of open-sided truck with a canopy was called a ranchero, and it was a common way to get around in the more remote stretches of South America.

As we bumped along the dusty roads, dirt clung to our sweaty skin and clogged our lungs. We held on to the seat backs in front of us as we jostled our way down the track, dense green foliage imposing on the road at every turn. Every time the ranchero slowed we stuck our hands out the side of the truck and caressed the exotic flowers with our fingertips.

When we finally hopped down from the ranchero and grabbed our backpacks, we were well and truly in the middle of nowhere. The immigration office was a shack on a dirt road, and the agent inside was wearing a soccer jersey while a fan blew in the corner. There was a faded picture of the Virgin Mary in a cracked frame behind him, the de facto decoration for every business we'd seen in Ecuador. He stamped us out of the country, and we walked under the wooden bar across the bridge that represented the border between the two countries.

After a long day of travel, we had arrived in Peru, but we still had hours to go to reach Chachapoyas. At this point we began questioning our decision to go through this remote overland border. Sure, it would lead us to pre-Incan ruins and some of the greatest walking in South America, but it was also incredibly remote. We'd see a 6th century fortress that rivaled Machu Picchu in size and historical importance. It was rediscovered in the 1980s, and there was a reason it stayed undiscovered for so long. This fortress was so far off the beaten path most people didn't go there, even Peruvians.

The next day meant a trip by *collectivo*, or small bus, to the bigger city of Jaen, then on to the town of Bagua Grande. Here we were able to catch a shared taxi to Chachapoyas, finally arriving after 36 hours and seven forms of transportation from our beginning point in the town with the straw men and alien seekers. If remote was what we were after, we found it.

Every city in South America has a central plaza that usually houses the church, the government buildings, and restaurants. The scene is always picturesque, and Chachapoyas was no different. At the corner of the square near an Internet cafe we found an adventure tour company.

We were the least prepared trekkers in the history of the world, but thankfully we didn't realize it. When we walked into the office, we were instantly intrigued by a 4-day trek that included several stops for natural and historical sites plus the grand destination of the ancient hilltop fortress known as Kuelap. We could easily take a bus to visit it, but wouldn't a hike through history be better?

Northern Peru is famous for its excellent hiking, and finding one combined with history appealed to us. And four days couldn't be so hard, could it? We'd been walking in the Andes Mountains by then for three months, adjusting to the high altitude and losing weight from healthier eating and daily walking. Surely we could do this thing.

The salesman said the trek was doable for people of average fitness. We read into this what we wanted (and what he wanted) instead of asking him to clarify "average." So we signed up to leave the next morning with a small group of people for four days. We left everything we didn't need – laptops, sandals, nicer clothes – back at the hotel in storage. What we didn't know was that it was rainy season, meaning it could pour down buckets of water for hours at any given moment. We didn't have any rain gear. Also, we each had to carry part of the group's food and water for the next four days, which was tough to fit and balance since we'd only brought our overstuffed daypacks with us. And finally, the elevation climb for each day, a number we thought we could handle, was actually simply the high point, not the total elevation we'd be climbing. There were multiple ups and downs throughout the day, making the elevation gain a number we couldn't even imagine doing until we were actually doing it. What we signed up for was far more rugged than we realized, and we came into it woefully unprepared.

On day one we loaded up in the town square into a group of minivans. Our guide, Wilberto, was a 20-something graduate student in agriculture studies. He told us he'd had been climbing these mountains his whole life and could make the trek we were about to do in just one long day. He was wearing baggy gray sweat pants and a T-shirt with cheap tennis shoes, and I wondered how his feet were going to hold up. I should have been worrying about my own.

The van first took us to Pueblo de los Muertos, or City of the Dead. These rock houses were built into the side of a cliff to house the dead, and historians believe these ancestors were looking out over the valley to protect the residents. Whether the historians were romantics or not, we liked that idea.

Who's looking out for us, we wondered? Most people we knew and loved didn't know where we were from day to day. We didn't even have a cell phone. If we got lost or hurt in these mountains, how long would it take for anyone to know? There were moments, especially when walking in remote places, when we felt our isolation acutely. These were also the times we realized how much we depended on each other for more than just love.

If I were a more melodramatic soul, I'd compare us to pioneers, leaving our friends and family behind to strike out for a better life out West. But since we had a guide and plenty of food and water, that would be a foolish comparison. Still, there was a feeling of kinship with other people who've chosen to leave what they know. By stepping into the unknown together, we had an automatic expectation that we were in this together, no matter what, and no matter how high tempers flared. We were all we had, and we realized this almost every day.

The walk down the dusty trail was hot and there was no shade, but the van waited at the top for our return in a couple of hours. I wondered if this "trek" was really just driving us from place to place for long walks. (Not that I hated that idea, but I knew Warren would.) Once the guide let us through the locked gate to the pueblos, we had to climb up to get there, finally scrambling over large boulders in a pretty ungainly manner to see the cliffside dwellings. A man gave me a boost up, and I wondered how the tiny Peruvian people of old made their way up here.

Warren walked out to the furthest point of the crumbling ruin, right to the tiniest ledge of stability, and I almost peed in my pants. It wasn't called the City of the Dead for nothing. He's always so daring in these situations and I am decidedly less so. He wants to see everything inside out, exploring every single crevice and surface. He pokes at things, picks them up, and turns them over. Sometimes he even breaks things. I am more of an observer, stepping back to see it from all angles. These differences perfectly explain our personalities. Warren is intense, in your face, and jumping forward into life. He doesn't take in as many details because he focuses in on the few most important things. I am more of an observer, looking at how everything links together and creates the entire environment. My head is full of details, so much so that sometimes I miss the main point.

When we fight, this difference comes out in what we call the "gym/hallway" conflict. I wander into a discussion as if walking into a big gym, looking up and around at the problem from every angle. Warren walks down a narrow hall, focusing on the one specific point in the discussion he wants to resolve. He gets frustrated when I don't hone in on the one thing he wants to decide, and I get mad when he won't talk about the problem in a more holistic manner. He thinks I'm clouding the issue with details, and I think he's making an uninformed decision by skipping those details.

We're both right.

At the time of the trek, I was thinking about his enthusiasm, his focus on the one detail (*Ruins! Look! I'm standing on history!*). I observed from the sidelines thinking about everything from what our ancestors would think about what we're doing to whether he was going to fall to his death. That's the difference between us, and it plays out every single day in such an obvious way that I'm astounded we didn't notice it before we began traveling. What we've come to appreciate about our differences is that Warren's focus and enthusiasm gets us into a scenario, and my attention to detail and nuance is what helps us process the experience. When we work together this way, the results are brilliant. When we don't, the situation is disastrous.

I wasn't sure which direction this trek was going to take.

After about an hour of exploring the pueblos and Warren teetering on the edge of the cliff we began the trek back down and up, stopping to see the magnificent Gocta Waterfall, rumored to be one of the highest in the world. We drove to lunch at a local restaurant. As we sat down to a hot meal and had the luxury of using flush toilets afterward, I was feeling surprisingly good. If this was trekking, I was all for it.

Next was the Sarcophagi de Karajia, which are human-shaped clay tombs that look like they are standing at attention on the cliff. At first we thought they were just statues, but we found out the dead were interred inside these clay tombs to watch over the living. It gave me a little shiver to think about it. Coming from a small town, I'd had enough of people nosing into my business. No need to survey my ancestors for their opinions.

After the walk back to the van, we took a beautiful drive through winding mountain roads and wispy fog to arrive at a lone house sitting in a lush, green valley. A stream snaked through the valley floor, and horses were grazing in the distance. It was beautiful and silent.

The ten of us got out as Wilberto began unloading our bags and the food and water. The driver and van then sped off into the fading sun, leaving us all alone. My hope of being driven from walk to walk was crushed; it was all on foot from this point forward. We helped Wilberto carry the gear to the small house, which was basically a tiny kitchen, a rustic bathroom, and a dorm room of bunk beds. There was no heat, no lock on the door, and only one small bare bulb in the sleeping room.

Wilberto set to work gathering wood, and soon we had a roaring campfire and makeshift seats created from large rocks and stray boards. The evening was getting cold already, and the fire was a good excuse for a bunch of strangers to start getting to know each other, especially given the time we'd be spending together over the next few days. Wilberto brought a fishing pole, and as we sat around the campfire we watched him cast into the stream. He didn't catch anything, but he said he was sure he would the next morning and we'd have fish for dinner. This comment caught my attention, as it implied that he didn't already have food ready for our dinner. Were we going to rely on Mother Nature to provide our food every night? There were no stores or restaurants nearby, and as he pointed out the path we'd take the next morning, through the valley and over the mountains, I was sure we wouldn't be passing any.

Early the next morning we had breakfast at the picnic table as Wilberto outlined our route. We'd be walking along the valley floor, crossing the icy cold stream in our bare feet, and then walking straight uphill and down the other side before stopping for the night. The morning was still, the mountain peaks covered with clouds and the green valley dotted with horses. As we started walking along the valley floor, Wilberto would stop on occasion and pull out his fishing pole and drop it in the water. He reeled in trout like a pro, securing them in a plastic bag to his backpack. I was both impressed and relieved, knowing we'd be ravenous at the end of the day.

At the edge of the valley we started a steep climb, and eventually we were in the clouds we'd seen from the valley floor. Wisps of fog swirled at our feet with every step on the mossy ground. No one spoke as we walked through this magical place, as if uttering one word would break the spell. Our legs were aching from the climb, but the singing birds hiding just beyond sight in the lush forest easily distracted us.

During our lunch break, as we ate bread, cheese, and chocolate on large boulders in the forest, Wilberto asked if we wanted to take a short detour to see a ruin that had not yet been excavated. The walled city was covered in vines, and it was tricky navigating our way down, tripping over roots as big as a man's thigh. But the reward was like being in our own Indiana Jones movie, seeing a pre-Incan city and imagining that villagers still lived there. Wilberto said the mountain was dotted with these ruins, too numerous for the Peruvian government to excavate. As we made our way around the wall of the city and back to our route, the skies opened and a true jungle rain poured down. We clustered together against the ancient wall of the city, imagining all the people in centuries before us who'd been caught in the rain in this very place.

It continued raining, but as it lessened we made our way back to where we'd eaten lunch and finally started the descent. The steep path was a river of mud, and for two hours we slid, fell, and trudged down. Warren's years of playing soccer made his legs strong and nimble, and he navigated this part far better than I did. Our bags were getting soaked and dirty, and because we didn't bring any rain gear or backpack covers, so were we. Every other person on our tour wore a poncho or rain gear and covered up their backpacks. We felt so dumb.

By the time we arrived at the bottom, the rain started letting up. We were filthy, tired, and wet. But most of all, we were starving. Wilberto led us to an L-shaped dwelling with a giant round clay oven in the courtyard. Dogs and chickens roamed around, and a short man and his wife came out to greet us. He was a baker, and he provided bread to the families who lived in the area, though we couldn't see any other houses. He had three rooms with double beds set up for trekkers like us as well as a modern outhouse. On the short side were his family quarters plus the kitchen, all with packed dirt floors.

We found our room and stripped off our wettest clothes. Almost everything we had in our packs was wet, and with the rain continuing to fall, that was not good news. Wilberto suggested we lay our clothes on top of the clay oven to dry, and we put our boots on wooden planks inside the oven. It was an ingenious solution. Everyone else came prepared with rain gear and plastic wrapped clothes inside their bags, and we again felt like idiots. Who goes on a trek in the rainy season without rain gear? We were so ill prepared, and it made the hardships even worse. Everyone was struggling because the walk was challenging, but they were able to recover at the end of the day in dry clothes and sandals, while we were still feeling the pain of wet clothes and soggy socks.

In stressful and embarrassing situations like this, it's easy to turn on each other. We could have blamed the other person for not thinking of something essential, like plastic bags, or for dragging us on this godforsaken trek in the first place. We still had 48 hours to go, and with damp clothes we knew it wasn't going to be easy. Instead of snapping at each other, we simply focused on what needed to be done to make the situation better, which was to put as many clothes as we could on the oven, put our boots inside, eat a big meal, and rest our tired bodies for the night. This lesson seems so obvious, but it's not the reality we lived for many years. Traveling put us in situations that required immediate action and focus. We lost the luxury of having the time and space to turn on each other.

We sat in the tiny dining room of the baker's house and looked inside the kitchen as his wife began preparing the fish Wilberto caught. The baker brought us some of his yucca bread along with a big tin of instant coffee and we all played cards as the dog sniffed around our feet and the chickens roamed in and out. The rooms were fairly dim, but even so we could see into the kitchen and notice scuffling around the floor with the occasional glint of an eye. Had we not already known guinea pigs were a diet staple in Peru for hundreds of years, we would have thought they were rats.

Just like their ancestors did, the baker's family kept these "free-range" guinea pigs in the kitchen. They mostly stayed beneath the kitchen worktable, munching on lettuce and other food scraps. During the cold mountain nights, the guinea pigs slept in a little cubby next to the wood-burning stove to stay warm. These guys lived pretty cushy lives until it came their turn to be the main course. We'd seen these roasted guinea pigs outside restaurants for months, turning on spits with head and tails attached, teeth bared, looking like vicious squirrels caught mid-run up the tree. While culturally fascinating, I was glad we had fish for dinner.

After a warm night's sleep, we woke up and put on our still damp clothes. I wasn't sure we were going to make it. My legs ached with every step, and I thought mold might be growing on me. Even Warren, the fitter of us, was sore. As tough as the uphill had been, the downhill in the muddy rain was one of the hardest things we'd ever done. Could our bodies take another day of this?

We set off for the most grueling climb we'd done to that point, stopping frequently for chocolate and water to break the intensity. I thought I was going to die. I remembered that our travel insurance had a rescue policy, and I wondered what constituted a big enough emergency for a helicopter lift. Then I thought about just stopping, dropping my pack and refusing to go further. But then I realized that meant staying the night in the jungle by myself, which was a pretty good motivator to keep moving. We'd go up 1000 meters, then down 1000 meters. There was precious little flat walking. Every time we started to walk down, I appreciated the break but knew we'd pay for it with another difficult ascent.

At noon we reached a fog-covered cliff with a small house and a gazebo looking out over the valley below. It reminded us of a Middle Earth scene, something out of *The Lord of the Rings*. As the fog moved through we could see the mountains across the valley. We sat at a long table overlooking the valley to eat a homemade lunch of soup, chicken, and the ever-present instant coffee. Wilberto treated us to another round of chocolate bars afterward, and we left to head into the final stretch of the day's walk.

Most people kept to themselves on the last leg of the trek, partly due to the tremendous exertion, and partly due to the magnificent beauty and peacefulness of the surroundings. It somehow seemed appropriate for each of us to enjoy this section by ourselves. Warren stayed near the lead, talking with Wilberto. As usual, his focus was on connecting with other people. I stayed nearer the back, often walking out of sight of the others, completely alone in this mystical space.

The clouds swirled around our feet, the toucans chattered in the distance, and we marveled at our surroundings and at the nearness of our accomplishment. It was a grueling nine hours of walking and climbing, the intense effort rewarded by lush foliage, towering peaks, and exotic birds.

At the top of the final peak Wilberto promised us an easy two-hour journey downhill to our destination. Downhill didn't have the same appeal to us after the previous day's muddy descent, but it was a welcome change from the continual climbing. Warren was still fairly energetic, but I was at the end of my energy level. As I came over the peak and saw the road, my heart soared. The tour company van was there and a driver leaned against hood smoking a cigarette. I started crying.

Wilberto gave us the option to ride down to the village or take the two-hour walk down, and our group split in half. I chose the van, and Warren chose the walk. I sat on a log outside a small store drinking a sugary soda and eating chocolate, stuffing calories into my depleted body as I waited for Warren to arrive.

That night we sat at a big table with the rest of our group, toasting with cold Pilsen beers to our accomplishment. We ate with gusto and then shuffled back to our rooms, feeling the day's effort in every step.

The next morning, we arrived at the fortress of Kuelap. As the van loads of day trippers arrived in the parking lot, we overheard a couple bickering in Spanish. We high-fived ourselves for making it the long way without fighting, which we immediately regretted due to our screaming muscles.

It might have taken us days to get over the soreness, but the thrill of accomplishment never went away.

12

Our Ship Comes In

Nine pilot whales swam in the ocean outside our porthole, and the only reason we saw them was that our ship was listing at a 44-degree angle into the sea every 30 seconds. Our upper deck cabin was transformed into an underwater viewing chamber. As amazing as it was to see these giant creatures swimming serenely underwater while the storm raged above, I couldn't appreciate it. The impact of this storm on my body was like a hangover turned inside out. The room was literally spinning, and I was the one that was still. The storm raged for hours, tossing us around like rag dolls. The captain had long ago sent all passengers and nonessential crew to their quarters.

I spent much of the storm following the captain's orders, nestled in my twin bed with giant wedge-shaped cushions on either side of me so I wouldn't roll out as the ship was tossed about in the waves. My main goal was to not throw up, because that meant leaving the relative safety of my bed and crawling to the toilet. And once there, I had to be careful of the door, which slammed shut every time it was opened due to the rocking and rolling of the ship. Nothing remained in place that wasn't already bolted down. Warren, who struggled with seasickness at the start of our journey when seas were relatively calm, seemed oblivious to the effects of bouncing through the sea and strapped himself into a chair to take photos from the lounge.

We were on our way back from an incredible two-week trip to Antarctica on board a small cruise ship of about 120 passengers. It was an active trip, with two landings via Zodiac motorboat every day to see the penguins, seals, and icebergs of Antarctica. We were still in the first six months of our travels, and it was the most incredible thing we'd done. We even camped overnight on the ice with about 15 other hearty souls.

Strangely, we were never afraid of anything bad happening during the storm, especially after going through the safety drills at the start of the cruise. I was too sick to be scared, and Warren was too excited by the experience.

Long after the storm was over and we were able to eat, sleep, and walk upright again, we learned one of the engines had stopped working during the storm. It made maneuvering the waves more difficult than it would normally be, which is why our ship was so easily tossed among the waves. Instead of meeting them head on, perpendicular fashion, and gliding through, we were bobbing side to side and getting the most motion possible. There was no patch or pill to combat that level of motion sickness.

Ships can only get to this frozen continent during a small window of time in the Antarctic summer when the ice breaks up enough to let them through. We were on the next-to-last cruise of the season, and despite the awful seasickness from the storm in the Drake Passage on our return – pegging out at a Force 12 on the Beaufort scale (hurricane force winds, for those who aren't sailors or weather geeks) - we were still in love with traveling by small ship. The crew joked with us later that if you have weathered a Force-12 storm, you can be so bold as to put your feet up on the dining room table in the finest homes in the world and no one will say a word. I'm sure that's more for the seafaring types than regular people, though.

The trip from Antarctica back to Ushuaia, Argentina, the southernmost city in the world, takes two days. We spent 18 hours of it locked into the storm, but afterward we enjoyed hours of calm seas and the return of the birds that followed our ship. As the nausea faded our minds were filled with the memories of blue icebergs, doddering penguins, and curious seals. If you asked us then to turn around and go back to Antarctica, we would have said yes. We would still say yes to this day.

I told Warren it would be really cool to cross the ocean in a ship like this some day. I didn't want to be on a huge cruise ship with thousands of people, but a smaller yet seaworthy vessel with about a hundred people and a crew you can get to know? That sounded terrific to me, and I hoped one day we'd be able to do it.

Warren immediately left our room to go talk to people, because that's what he does. I used to complain about it, but after what he did next I never will again. The hotel manager for the ship was a lovely Brazilian woman named Alessandra. We talked to her every day because the reception desk was near our cabin door. Warren asked her questions about the ship, just like he did the other crew members. He was fascinated to know more about the life they lived ten months a year away from their homes and families.

That day Alessandra told Warren they had only one more cruise to Antarctica for the season and she was going to miss it.

"What do you do next?" he asked.

Alessandra told him about the repositioning process and how they had to get the ship ready for the Arctic season up north. The ship would take a very slow trip up to England, about five and a half weeks long, while the crew performed maintenance. Carpets were shampooed, wallpaper was replaced, and the ship was painted inside and out. The harsh polar environment of these ships meant a constant state of maintenance. Warren remembered our conversation a few minutes earlier in the cabin and did the most incredible thing he's ever done:

"Can we come with you?"

He thought there was about a five percent chance she'd say yes, but it didn't hurt to ask. (It probably also doesn't hurt that Alessandra is a beautiful and funny young woman and any time spent talking to her was a bonus for him.) She wondered why we'd want to be on the ship if there were no stops, no entertainment, and with all that work going on around us. To her, it was work. To Warren, it was an adventure across the ocean and a way to make my dream come true. Alessandra agreed to contact her corporate office and see what the options were since they normally took no passengers during this time. He grinned the way he always does when he's got a plan in motion, and went looking for me.

"You did what?!" I couldn't believe he'd had such an outlandish idea and then followed through on it without even telling me. Part of me was overjoyed that he listened so closely to what I wanted, even in just a casual, dreamy conversation. The other part was impressed with his gumption. Then my overthinking brain kicked in and I remembered we had plans already to hike in Patagonia, to taste wine and see friends in Mendoza, and to finally climb Machu Picchu. If we went on this trip, we'd have to cancel all those plans.

While I'm not a planner by nature, I do dread disappointing people. Even more than that, I hate missing out on something I really want, and Machu Picchu was high on my list. For a brief moment, I mentally decided we couldn't go on the ship because of those plans.

Then it dawned on me. I was worrying for nothing. The ship owners hadn't agreed, for one thing. And even if they did, Machu Picchu, Mendoza, and Patagonia – in fact, all of South America – would still be there later. An opportunity to take a ship across the ocean as the only passengers likely would not be. The scenario reminded me of our problem at the start of the trip, when we didn't know whether to follow our carefully made plans and fly into a political coup attempt or go off-plan and do something else. The lesson was finally sinking in that we could do whatever we wanted, and making the most of opportunities at hand was far more important than following a plan set out weeks or months before when the opportunity was hidden. We didn't have to follow the rules; we could make our own.

This was when we first began solidifying our idea that life was not a series of right and wrong decisions. Instead, it was more like a flow chart. If we chose A, then the options flowed to C and D. If we choose B, then our options flowed to E and F, and so on. The important piece was not what option we chose but that we kept choosing. It was a Choose Your Own Adventure type of scenario, and we chose to throw our plans out the window and start making the most of what came our way.

We laughed a little at the entire situation, remarking on how this trip was turning out far different than we imagined. Not only that, we were learning skills we never knew we needed, in situations we never imagined happening. When we arrived back in Ushuaia, we bid farewell to Alessandra and the crew. She told us she'd email soon and let us know what the corporate office said, and we made plans to stick around Ushuaia for a while with a few of the travelers from the ship.

A few of us went camping together in Tierra del Fuego, a Dutch/Canadian/German/American crew of mostly neophyte hikers, waking up to icicles on our tents and busy beavers down below constructing a dam in the water. Winter was coming, and the small taste of it was more than enough to send us scurrying back to the warm hostel after just one night. It was here that we checked our email and learned the ship's main office was seriously considering our offer. After all, we had a popular blog and it would be good PR for them to have us write about the journey. Why not?

We had a call with the marketing manager, and we were excited to learn that we'd get free passage on the ship but have to pay our own bar tab. Smart people. Free Internet was also provided so we could blog and tweet about the adventure. We were so excited we could hardly stand it. It just didn't seem real.

Our last night in South America coincided with a super moon, when the moon makes its closest approach to earth in the lunar orbit. It was enormous, looming just over the horizon. We walked to a nearby hill to watch it rise into the night sky. The super moon is said to coincide with major natural events and tide changes, and the more woo-woo types claim it inspires the same kinds of emotional and mental eruptions and breakthroughs in people. We awkwardly joked about what could happen on a journey like this, but we thought luck was on our side after already going through the big storm on the way back from Antarctica. Still, we looked on the super moon as a good omen for our next adventure.

Standing outside on the dock with the anchor chain high up above, even a small ship can seem huge. This ship was a red and white beauty, and we stood staring at it for a while. I had a fleeting thought that we had the date wrong, or that something was going to fall through before we set sail. It just seemed so weird to be the only people on the dock. But the gangway was down so we began climbing up, hoping our bunks were ready.

There were a few crew members at the landing, including Alessandra. We expected to bunk and eat with the crew, so it surprised us when she led us up to the fourth deck, which was where we stayed before. Then she took us to the corner cabin, a two-room suite, and opened the door. Was this a tour of the ship, starting with the top and then working us down to our lowly bunks? Because if it was, that seemed like a bad idea.

She told us to drop our bags so we could continue the tour. We smiled at each other as we realized we'd spend the next 37 days in a suite on a ship crossing the ocean with our own personal attendant. Alessandra then took us to the dining room, where the head chef asked us when we wanted to eat our meals every day.

"Whenever everyone else eats is fine with us," we said. We expected to adhere to a set schedule of kitchen hours, not to be dictating to the crew.

Chef told us we'd be eating proper meals in the dining room every day with a menu. Crazy to think we'd have the entire dining room to ourselves three times a day. We went back to our room to unpack and planned to watch the departure from the upper deck, waving goodbye to South America. When we arrived in our room, we found tea and cookies in the living room area of our suite. This journey was going to be completely different from what we expected, which was starting to be the constant in our lives.

The next few weeks were some of the most relaxing and enjoyable we'd ever spent. Every night the ship rocked us to sleep with gentle motion. The food was outstanding. After breakfast each morning, I wrote about our travels so far, including what we were learning about life on the ship, from a desk looking out at the sea. Warren spent his mornings on the bridge learning about the workings of a ship from the officers. In the afternoons our attendant delivered tea and fresh-baked cookies from the kitchen. We sat outside as the weather got warmer, watching dolphins leaping, flying fish that looked like fairies, and the occasional whale pod.

At night, we'd stroll up to the top deck and lie down next to the smokestack to watch the blanket of stars come out. There were more stars than we had ever seen (even topping the mountain view in the Andes). The Southern Cross was on vivid display in the inky blackness of the sky over the indigo blue of the sea.

When we weren't writing, learning about the ship, eating, or reading, we were lucky to hang out with the staff after they finished working. Several of them pooled their money and bought a karaoke machine for downtime, and during repositioning cruises they move the machine to the main lounge. Every week, we took the stage and belted out tunes with the mostly Filipino crew, learning traditional songs like *Pinoy Ako* and crooning our own favorites, songs from Carly Simon and Johnny Cash. We felt deliciously silly, probably the most lighthearted and relaxed we'd ever been.

In what was perhaps Warren's most incredible act of persuasion, he convinced the well-mannered crew to lip-sync to the snarky song *I'm On a Boat*, while he recorded on video. The song was made famous by

Saturday Night Live alumnus Andy Samberg and the rapper T-Pain. Warren had a great time choreographing the crew, even convincing the chef to stand Titanic style on the bow of the ship in his tall white hat. Everything about that trip was lighthearted and fun.

The time on the ship was good for us. We got to see life in a completely different way, learning about what it takes to work on a ship as well as hearing the crew's stories from their native lands. For the first time since we left Ecuador, we didn't have to pack and unpack every few days or arrange transportation and lodging. We didn't have to wonder about where to go and what to do. We had plenty of time to process what the previous six months had done for our relationship.

The cruise all started from me saying what I wanted, no matter how outlandish it my have seemed, and Warren remembering it and seizing an opportunity when he saw it. One of the lessons we've learned as we've traveled the world is making each other's small and large dreams come true is well worth the effort. The memories last forever, unlike trinkets and material possessions. And saying what you want, no matter how unusual, has a better chance of getting to yes than just wishing.

13

A Dictator and a Manipulator

"Americans at the back!" The bartender at our "local" jerked his thumb toward the dark wood back booth as we walked in. Even under our jackets and wool caps, we were recognizable. He started pulling two real ales for us before we even had our jackets off. We smiled, realizing we were becoming regulars in our little neighborhood in Edinburgh, Scotland.

After crossing the Atlantic, we spent some time traveling around the UK, eventually ending up in Edinburgh and deciding to stay a while. Another traveler we knew online connected us with the landlord of a small apartment, and we rented it for five weeks. During our few weeks already we'd made friends with the gregarious Scots, going out to pubs, storytelling nights, dinner parties, and even climbing small mountains on the West Coast with a local hill walking group.

In one of our first experiences of speaking the same language but not understanding, our English friends told us the Scots were mean people. We took that to mean disagreeable and unfriendly, so we were surprised to meet such a friendly group. In fact, the Scots are pranksters with a great sense of humor. On our Facebook page, a friend of a friend reached out to say she lived near Edinburgh and would love to show us around. We arranged to meet at Cafe Royale, just across the North Bridge from the Royal Mile, at 2:00 p.m. Her name was Joan, and all we knew was that she had brown shoulder-length hair and had a great sense of humor.

There were four men at the bar when we arrived, and they looked to be longtime friends. I walked up to order our drinks and asked them what they were having. They recommended the stout and then welcomed us to Scotland after hearing my accent. It was a far cry from what I was expecting after what our English friends told us, and I shared this with them. "A mean person has arms that won't reach his pockets," our new friends at the bar told us with a laugh as they paid for our drinks. In American English "mean" is cruel or spiteful. In the Queen's English "mean" is just cheap! This was the first of many "we're not speaking the same language" moments we had in the UK.

A little while later Joan still hadn't arrived, so I walked around the restaurant to make sure we hadn't missed her. We decided to have another drink and wait, so I went back to the bar to order another round and buy one for the generous men who'd welcomed us to Scotland. I didn't want to be "mean," you know. As the bartender pulled the beers, I began telling them why we were there. They were intrigued when I told them we met Joan online, at first thinking it was some kind of swinger's club hookup. It took a minute to explain what was going on, and by the time I finished telling the story, we hatched a plan to prank Joan. She was already 45 minutes late, so we decided when she came through the door, these four gentlemen would rush toward her in greeting, acting like long-lost friends, while we waited at the corner table.

Joan finally breezed in, starting her apologies to the mostly empty room as soon as she walked in the door. It was obvious being late was not a new thing for her. She was surprised to have these men at the bar stand up and yell, "Joanie, we've missed you, lass!" They then loudly ordered her favorite drink, a gin and tonic, and the youngest swept her up in a giant bear hug and swung her around. "The party can't start 'til you arrive, Joan!"

Joan started laughing and realized we were behind the prank as we walked up behind her new friends. That was the start of an evening that lasted almost eight hours. Joan eventually introduced us to a large circle of friends and family during our stay, and we enjoyed the kind of experience you can only have when you know the locals. It's probably why we love this city so much and keep returning.

Back at our "local," which is what the Scots call their local neighborhood pub, we took off our jackets and settled into our booth. We thought about our success in meeting people and how it quickly made any location feel like home. The key was staying long enough to meet the local people and make friends. Our experience told us we'd likely continue feeling "at home" around the world no matter where we went as long as we continued reaching out and making friends. And if we could make temporary homes all over the world, was there a reason to go back to the U.S. and make a home again?

The next thought gave us goose bumps: Could we be temporary residents of countries all over the world? If so, we'd need a lot more time and money than we booked for this crazy little adventure.

"I don't ever want this to end," I said.

The bartender set down our pints and said, "Ye'd best finish this one first."

We smiled at the joke, but Warren at least knew what I meant. He'd been thinking the same thing, and we arrived at the pub with notebook in hand to see how we could extend our travels indefinitely.

We fell back to our tried and true method of making dreams come true by asking ourselves these questions: What do we really want? What does that look like on a daily basis? When do we want it to start? Working backward, what do we need to do now and every day forward to make that happen?

What we wanted was a way to continue seeing the world and sharing our experiences with our family, friends, and fellow midlife reinventionists. Realistically, that required a regular income, doing work that was not dependent on time zone or location, and probably online. We'd have to be able to carry our work with us in our backpacks. We'd probably have to do more of what we were doing in Edinburgh, becoming short-term residents instead of travelers to give us the stability to work and time to explore. While we still had savings, we knew the money wouldn't last forever and the smart bet would be to build an income now, long before we ran out of cash.

What we mapped out that day in our notebook as we sipped our beer and ate steak pies was the start of the next phase of our dream. The trip turned into a lifestyle in that moment. But of course planning was just the first step in making a change, and we knew from past experience that immediate action was vital to keep the momentum going. If we sat on this idea too long, it would fade and we'd never make it happen. When the money ran out, we'd be very limited in our options, and we never wanted to feel that way again.

We thought about our website, Married with Luggage, and the community of readers we'd built up since we first made our decision to quit our jobs, sell everything we owned, and travel the world in 2008. People asked us every week how we did it – "it" being everything from saving money to getting rid of our stuff to spending so much time together without killing each other. We loved writing for the site, sharing our experience and insights along the way. From childhood I'd wanted to be an author, writing books and sharing my words with the world. With the website I got a tiny taste of that dream, but the one novel I did write never saw the light of day. It was terrible, and I convinced myself I would never write seriously.

But the articles on our site did get a lot of attention, and people seemed to like them. I never stopped wanting to write, and Warren always encouraged me to take it up again. As we sat there thinking about what we could do next, Warren asked me again if I wanted to write for a living. Would people actually read a book about our experience and lessons? We weren't sure, but we decided to try it and see.

Working together was initially very exciting. Ideas were flowing, we were making plans and envisioned success. But when it came to the real work – getting our hands dirty – we came to the surprising conclusion that we had very different ways of doing it.

Warren is blunt. He gets to the point as quickly as efficiently as he can, and he's always focused on the next action we can take. He is deadline-driven and results-oriented. He's always looking at the big picture and is typically a few steps ahead of most everyone else in the room, including me. He's swayed by facts, not feelings, and he values the success of the project over anyone's ego. He's the definition of a problem-solver.

I am much more of a consensus builder. My skills are in creating strong networks of people and taking the long view of success in any project. I convince and convert through team-building and words, and though my vision is not as sharp, my powers of persuasion are strong. I'm not as much swayed by sterile facts as I am input from other team members. I don't go by gut, but I don't ignore it, either. I am the definition of a team leader.

Match these two personalities up and what you get is a dictator and a manipulator (if you believe the worst of our tendencies). And when we mixed our business and personal lives together, this difference came to a head on many occasions. I didn't want to be bossed around, and Warren didn't want me to talk him into anything.

I hated Warren's negativity and thought it brought down our creativity. He hated my "bright side" perspective because he thought it masked problems. Warren critiqued my writing as if I were a subordinate, not the woman he was hoping to sleep with each night. I resented being told by him what was wrong with my writing and generally ignored his feedback. He would tell me we were having these conversations as business partners, not life partners, and I should have a different attitude. My attitude was that we were partners period and we should always interact that way. There were a lot of bumps in our early days of working together.

I once read a book about birth order and how it influences habits and attitudes. Oldest children tend to be the leaders and achievers, working hard for approval from their parents and often taking the role of "mini mom or dad" to the younger siblings. As oldest children grow up, they translate this "bossy" attitude to friends, coworkers, and lovers. Middle children are the peacemakers, and youngest children are the entertainers and ones typically free of the burden of feeling responsible for everything. This is an oversimplification, of course, but like many stereotypes it has a grain of truth. Both Warren and I were first borns, and we both wanted to call the shots.

A few months after our decision to make Married with Luggage into a proper business we finished our first book, *Dream Save Do: An Action Plan for Dreamers*. This was before Kindle was as hot as it is today, and we decided to publish it as a PDF eBook on our own site on October 15, 2011. I remember this date mainly because we were sitting on the floor of a rental condo in Chiang Mai, Thailand, delirious adjusting to the time change after flying in from Europe just two days before, and struggling with an internet connection that kept going down.

Every time we fixed one problem in the layout of the book, another one popped up. We were tired, grumpy, and getting on each other's nerves. The new bed was as hard as a rock, and the heat outside was intense. We didn't speak the language, and we'd been working for every hour we'd been awake to meet the deadline we'd already promoted to the public. The book launch we imagined, clicking the "upload" button in sunny Thailand as we lay back in our lounge chairs sipping fruity drinks and relishing the new role of authors, remained a dream. Our "glamorous" life was anything but in that moment, and we were fighting about important things and stupid things with equal intensity.

We had to create a better way of working together.

The answer was simple, logical, and overlooked in our desire for dominance. We had to take separate roles. Once we agreed on a direction or a project and mapped out our roles, we had to stop nagging, controlling, checking up, and second-guessing. We had to trust that the other was doing their job.

We split up our duties, taking responsibility for things that fell within our strengths. We became the bosses of our own realms of expertise and deferred to the other for theirs. For weaknesses we shared, like designing book covers, we hired subcontractors. And to keep us on track, we had a single weekly meeting to get status updates and a shared calendar of to-dos so we could see where the other one was in relation to our own tasks.

The more we worked "separately together," the better we got at it. The book income wasn't enough to sustain us yet, but we were on our way. People wanted to read our books, and sales went up every month. The word was getting out.

Then the emails started. Some were cheery and happy, some were tragic but hopeful, and others were lists of excuses why they couldn't do what we proposed. We were obviously touching some nerves.

People liked our straightforward attitude and conversational style about making big changes. For the first time, I realized our message and experience could really help people. Sharing stories about the incredible people we met along our travels could help people. Just telling people it was okay to change, to move, to go against the flow, could help.

If there was a type of business we wanted, this was it. And we set out to track not only our sales, but also the success stories that came from them. Married with Luggage was officially in business, and I achieved my childhood dream of being an author several times over.

14

Rules of Fighting

"Why do you have to be such an incredible asshole?"

The sun was shining, the birds were singing, and we were surrounded by lush green trees on a remote trail next to a stream. If we didn't hate each other so much at the moment, it would have been paradise. We were just 15 minutes into a 12-mile walk back to our flat in Edinburgh. That morning we'd boarded a bus with our backpacks, sack lunches, and water, to be dropped off at the trailhead 12 miles away. We had only our feet to get us down the long, meandering path home.

I had our water and the key to the apartment we'd rented in the Leith Walk area of Edinburgh, Scotland. Warren had the food and money. We couldn't split up even if we wanted to – and we definitely wanted to. The day started so well, and we were looking forward to this walk after working so hard on our first book and officially launching our business. It was an exciting time for us, and I was anxious to reconnect as lovers instead of just business partners. Walking together in nature was one way we always did that. So why was he being such an asshole?

I felt like I'd been ambushed. And then I was forced to talk it out over the next several hours as we made our way home. Inside I was steaming, mad at Warren and mad at myself for not packing the key and money together in my pack so I could just get the hell out of there.

As we walked along this gorgeous trail with a stream flowing beside us, birds chirping, and the occasional dog walker or jogger saying a friendly hello, I thought it was really crappy of Warren to start a fight. He was ruining this beautiful experience for both of us, one that I was not going to be keen to do again. But I could sense his hurt, even through my anger, and I knew it was a big moment. We had to work through this problem that had been building, and that meant facing my own shortcomings.

I thought back to that marriage counselor we saw in Massachusetts and how unproductive the sessions were. If only he'd given us talking points and dropped us 12 miles outside of town!

At first Warren couldn't pinpoint why he was so mad. He was fuming at nothing in particular, so he pulled out every irritant he'd ever had. I didn't take our business seriously. I didn't want sex often enough. I didn't make enough decisions about our travel. I didn't talk enough. I slept too late.

I stood slack-jawed as he railed against me, my ancestors, and everything I'd touched since birth. And the more he played the blame game, the less I listened. I was pretty sure after about 30 minutes of his haranguing that my husband was insane.

I pointed out that if I were such a horrible partner, perhaps he'd like to ditch me and find another one. Then he told me I was too defensive. I told him I had to be since he was always on the attack, blurting out every single thought that crossed his mind. If I did that, I'd never stop talking. At this he stopped in his tracks, wanting to know what I wasn't saying.

It was a disaster of a fight, and it was indicative of the difference in our personalities. I don't want to air every single grievance, preferring to let some things slide in the interest of preserving our personalities. I certainly don't want to be called out on stupid things like how I load the dishwasher, so I don't do it to other people.

Warren, on the other hand, is always looking to improve himself. If I critiqued the way he loaded the dishwasher, he'd show me either why I was wrong or he'd accept my way of doing it. He feels that way about every subject. It is exhausting to me, as much as my silence on these kinds of subjects is infuriating to him.

It took a while to hone in on the reason he was so upset. It was my negativity. As I said "hell, yeah!" to everything on the surface, I was backdooring it with negative comments. "Sure we can do that, but don't forget the *blahdyblahblah* that will likely ruin our lives and push us into bankruptcy." I thought I was being funny. Warren was being pelted with my negativity every day, and instead of speaking up he kept pushing it down. I didn't realize I was coming across so harsh and even prided myself on my quirky sense of humor.

"Let's go swimming! But hey, watch out for the killer shark that is likely lurking under the surface."

The fight had been simmering for a while, but neither one of us picked up on it. We had a few small fights in the weeks leading up to it, and I thought Warren was just being nit-picky because of our straining budget in such an expensive part of the world. He was continually dissatisfied because the real issue was never brought to the table and resolved, and I was keeping my distance emotionally to give him space to deal with what I thought was his issue. We each continued to make the problem worse by following this pattern.

When the problem finally came to light, after I made a comment about hoping we brought enough water for the walk, he exploded. And with it came every instance of my negativity over the past few months. He finally said it, and I finally got it. We were on the same page for the first time in weeks.

We stopped in a field about halfway through the walk and shared our lunch. The yelling was over, and we were numb in the way you get after a big fight. One of us made an awkward joke about whether we could trust the other to hold both the key and the money now that lunch was consumed. It was still tricky, so we thought it best to keep the vital supplies split between us. Sometimes being forced to stay together is a good thing.

By the time we reached Edinburgh, we came to a truce. The pressure was gone, and we were both a little raw from the accusations and revelations on our walk. We both had work to do, but being able to see the problem clearly meant we could fix it.

This 12-mile marriage therapy session taught us three things. The first was that we can't resolve a fight if we don't know what it's about. The grab-bag approach of pulling out every mistake or wrong word the other has said simply clouds the issue and increases the anger and resentment. It feels good in the moment, but it doesn't accomplish anything in the long term and guarantees we'll fight about the same subject again and again. We decided at the end of that day to only fight about one thing at a time from that point forward.

We also learned to assume the best intentions of each other. Rather than thinking I was a negative jerk, Warren tried to see it from the best light. Was it a weird sense of humor, or was there something else lurking that was making me this way? Better to find out the source than lash out at the symptom. In the same way, I learned not to get angry over his delivery of a complaint and focus more on the intention. He wanted to solve the problem so we could be happier.

Perhaps the best lesson we learned, though, was to end the fight on a humorous note. Fights often dragged out for us, with resentment lasting hours or even days. With a business to run together and often relying on each other exclusively in our travels, we had to find a quick way to get back to normal.

Warren came up with the best parting line: "Are we ready to have sex yet?" And my response: "Not if you want to keep all your parts."

This little chuckle showed life was back to normal and we could start the loving again.

15

Roughed Up in a Thai Prison

The prisoner knelt behind Warren and grabbed him by the neck. His head dropped forward, almost in a prayer-like position, and I knew what was coming next. I tensed up in anticipation, almost as if it were happening to me, while he sleepily drooped his head and gave in. *Crack!* I could hear his neck pop from across the room.

"Ahhhhhh." The moan of relief was audible, and the women in the room giggled. Warren looked up and said, "Kob kun krab." This made them giggle more. These women in pink pajamas were all prisoners at the Chiang Mai Women's Correctional Institute in Thailand. The spa was part of a vocational program to transition prisoners out into society with job skills after release. We were there with our British friends Chris and Hilary, who came to see us in this sunny country to escape part of the rainy winter in England.

The four of us wore the traditional pajamas for a Thai massage and lay on low beds on the floor separated by pink, filmy curtains. The room was light and airy, and the only indication we were in a prison was that we had to check in with an armed guard instead of a receptionist for our appointment. The four of us grunted and moaned our way through the 90-minute massages given by these petite criminals, marveling at the strength in such small bodies. My masseuse was easily half my weight, yet she still managed to lift me up by the back with her feet, shaking loose the last bit of tightness I had left in my body.

When it was over, we floated our way to the sterile waiting room with the linoleum floor, in full sight of the guard, while the prisoners brought us the traditional tea. Warren again said, "kob kun krab," the masculine form of "thank you" in Thai. Everywhere we traveled he tried to learn a bit of the language, and in Thailand he was making good progress. The women giggled and gently corrected his pronunciation as he asked them about where they were from and what they planned to do upon release. We marveled that these women were convicted criminals. After seeing movies like *Brokedown Palace*, which showed the grittiest kind of prison life in Thailand, this gentler image didn't quite compute.

But so many things in our travels didn't turn out as we expected. One in particular was the number of friendships we made when we thought our lifestyle would make it impossible to maintain them. Happily, we were wrong.

This was our third meet up with Chris and Hilary, after first meeting them in South America at a Happy Hour before our cruise to Antarctica. We were surprised to find ourselves just two doors down from each other a few days later on the ship.

We became fast friends, meeting every evening in their cabin for cocktails and sharing of pictures and stories from the day with a few other passengers. At the end of the trip, they invited us to stay with them in England anytime. Two months later we knocked on their door when we arrived in the U.K. on the same ship we'd all taken to Antarctica. We met their daughters, her parents, and a few friends. We took day trips and weekend trips together. We talked about the curve balls of life, aging parents, World War II – none of the light topics you'd normally expect in a new friendship. But we also watched *The Rocky Horror Picture Show* and played a silly card game called Shithead and baked bread together. It was a fast track to friendship that we eventually came to expect in this new lifestyle.

Superficial conversations don't last long amongst travelers. Time is short, and we're all seeking adventure, information, and experience. Future adventures are planned within hours or days of meeting, and personal information is exchanged as easily as other people talk about the weather. We'd never had such warm friendships develop so quickly in our lives, and we loved what it added to our relationship.

Chris and Hilary later came to visit us in Edinburgh, where we rented an apartment. We spent Warren's 40th birthday weekend driving around the gorgeous Scottish countryside together, making up dirty limericks. Now they were in Thailand, and we were joking about our four-continent friendship in the waiting room of a Thai prison.

Hilary has perhaps the sharpest and most analytical mind of anyone we know. She loves a good debate, and her tiny stature belies a fierce spirit. She and Warren could go round and round about any subject under the sun as long as Chris and I kept them fed and hydrated. She calls him on his nonsense, and holds his own with her commanding style. It is fascinating to watch, especially since both have a silly side as well. They are the ones who insist on the tradition of an outlandish "loser" hat when playing cards together.

Chris and I are the more light-hearted and easygoing counterparts to our mates. Without us, Warren and Hilary are a bit too intense. Without them, Chris and I are a bit too reserved. Each couple balances well on its own, but as a foursome there's an added dimension we don't have alone. This makes everyday experiences like cooking and more outlandish experiences like getting massages in a women's prison more enjoyable than they would be if we did them by ourselves.

Travel has forced us to evaluate new friendships quickly. If we're going to bond and stay in touch, we need to solidify the relationship in a matter of hours or days, weeks at the outside. After that, we've moved on and the odds of getting a second chance to become friends is small. This means deeper conversations on a faster time frame than we'd normally have with someone in our former lifestyle. We talk about love and death and politics and human rights and aging and all the other taboo dinner party subjects. Secrets are shared. People tell us things they haven't told their oldest friends, and we do the same. Being away from home creates a zone of safety, an "out of the norm" feeling that leads the way to a deep bond with people it would take us months or years to accomplish in our past.

These friendships give us something we don't get from each other. And if there's one thing we've learned after 24/7 togetherness since 2010, it's that you can't be all things to another person. Other people are essential to fill in the gaps and add to your experience. The burden is too great to attempt to fill every need of your partner, which is why new friendships should be developed throughout life.

We didn't always feel that way. In 2006 we were sitting in an outdoor cafe in Barcelona sipping sangria like all good tourists do, wondering what we should see next on our 10-day vacation. It was late fall, and tourism had dropped substantially, leaving us the only people in the café.

A couple in their early 50s came outside and made a beeline for our table. We both wondered why they would come over to sit so close to us when the entire place was empty, and we were doubly shocked when they stopped at our table and asked to join us.

"Uh, sure," was about all we could muster. *What kind of people do this?*

They were seasoned travelers, having been all over the world as they carved out an incredibly adventurous life in between their careers and rearing children in the US. We were fascinated by their stories, especially because they looked so average. We thought lifestyles like that only belonged to super-rich or glamorous people.

As we were winding up the conversation they asked where we lived and we told them, and they mentioned wanting to come to Seattle at some point. We told them they should, it was a great place, and of course we would love to see them if they did.

That's when it got awkward.

They gave us their contact information and asked for ours, and we hedged, saying we left our business cards back at the hotel. You see, we didn't actually mean it when we said we'd love to see them, at least not in the "let's make plans now" kind of way. Didn't we need more time to get to know each other first?

(Kind of a strange thought when you realize there was no more opportunity to get to know each other if we didn't exchange contact information.)

"How weird was that?" we said to each other afterward. "Can you imagine coming up to random strangers and then making plans with them so soon after meeting?" We failed to make the connection between their social habits and the incredible life they lived. Now we know that life is richer with other people in it, no matter how much you love your partner. But back then, we just thought it was weird.

When we left Barcelona, we emptied their contact information in the trash along with all our receipts and other loose paper. We shut the door on a new relationship before it even had a chance to start. We've come a long way since then.

Brussels Central Station smelled like waffles. After generally smelling burned coffee and *eau de urine* at most train stations around the world, this was a welcome change. We looked around for our contact, a woman named Alison with short red hair. She was our first house sitting client who wasn't a personal friend, and we weren't sure what to expect.

The gig came about through a friend of a friend, someone who saw Alison's post on a private Facebook traveler's group. She and her husband Andrew were looking for house and cat sitters at their Brussels condo while they made their annual trek back to Canada to visit family and friends. After a few messages back and forth, we were booked, arriving in Brussels via the Eurostar from London in the mid-afternoon.

Alison waved from platform, easily picking us out with our giant backpacks. We took another train back to her house, where we climbed the five flights of stairs to their apartment. The plan was to stay here for two nights as they showed us around the city and the cats got used to us, and then they were leaving for a month. The first night, they took us to a hidden gem of a French restaurant for dinner.

Over cassoulet and wine, the four of us talked about their lives as ex-pats in Belgium and how they adjusted to life in another country. We had more in common than we thought – books, travel, food, politics – and the dinner stretched into the late-night hours. The next night Alison cooked Flemish stew, which was a hearty meal made with Belgian beer and bread coated with mustard, slow cooked with meat over several hours until it melted on top of the famous

Belgian frites.

The conversation went again into the late hours of the night, until the last of the four jumbo orders of frites was gone and the stew was no more. Alison and Andrew didn't want to leave the next day, and we didn't want them to go.

After an enjoyable month eating and drinking our way through Brussels, they returned and we immediately made plans for a future meet up in Amsterdam. We tried the local specialty drink, jenever, from a 400-year-old bar and then ate spicy Mexican food as we dreamed up road trips around Europe and Asia. The relationship became a one-upmanship of how we could best support each other's crazy dreams. We've since met up multiple times in Brussels and even spent a month together in Morocco in a tiny apartment, cooking our spicy tagines on a hot plate and taking hundreds of pictures as we walked through old souks and medinas. Who knew that those 48 hours would lead to a deep friendship?

Andrew gave us business advice as he was earning his MBA. Alison read our second book before publication, providing excellent feedback to make it better. We brainstormed murder plots for Alison's mystery series. Warren and Alison shared world cuisine recipes.

We found another couple with whom we could be ourselves, sharing our greatest joys, deepest worries, and questions about the world. And we found these friendly Canadians in Belgium through an American friend on Facebook who was living in Berlin.

We've learned to open ourselves up to these tenuous connections, testing them for strength early on and fortifying the best ones as quickly as possible. These unlikely friendships add to our relationship in a way we couldn't possibly duplicate on our own, and we've repeated these successes with a dozen other lifelong friends around the world, not to mention many warm acquaintances.

Our most important friendship is with each other, no doubt, but the new friendships we gather to our life add to the richness of our experience. And that makes us better partners to each other.

Plus we've learned valuable life skills from these friends, like how to scan a limerick, plan a murder, remodel a house, climb a rock, prepare a curry, tell a story, take a photo, understand cricket, and eat bugs. We even know how to handle a prison inmate now, but only if she's wearing pajamas.

16

Smoking Spitting Pissing Pooping

The plan was simple. We'd leave Northern Thailand and take a road trip to Lisbon, Portugal, a mere 18,000 kilometers (11,200 miles) away. We didn't have a car, so we'd rely on buses and trains for much of the journey through Laos, China, Mongolia, Russia, and Europe. What could possibly go wrong?

China had long held our fascination, and we paid extra to get double-entry visas from the Chinese Embassy in Thailand so we could stay a full six months in this vast country. There were 5,000 years of history to uncover, and we were more excited than we'd been for any destination besides Antarctica. The Terra Cotta Warriors, thousands of life-sized clay figurines buried with the first Chinese emperor over 2000 years ago, were on our must-see list. We wanted to walk on the Great Wall, trek across Tiger Leaping Gorge, and visit the old hutongs of Xi'an and Beijing where families have lived together for centuries. As high school students in the late 1980s, we had a special interest in seeing Tiananmen Square, home of the protest of 1989. Who could forget the Forbidden City, especially after seeing the movie *The Last Emperor*? And pandas! We were excited to see pandas.

On April 1, 2012, we rushed forward like fools into our great road trip. We were heading north and then west, crossing Asia and Europe by the time we were done. It would take months to complete this journey at our pace, using only trains, buses, camels, horses, and our own two feet. We never dreamed it would be anything but fantastic, and much of that was due to our excitement over China.

The idea for the road trip started with a book I picked up six months before while visiting our friends in Belgium. It was the story of Genghis Khan, from childhood through his eventual domination of Asia, and it was mesmerizing. The book painted a picture of horses running free, grassy steppes, airy desert, and majestic mountains in what is now Russia, Mongolia, and China. I wanted to see it all, and Warren added a twist on our travels: we'd do it all overland without the use of planes.

Day one of our journey took us by minibus to the border of Laos. The Mekong River separated Thailand and Laos, which meant a short journey in a long, narrow boat across the muddy water to the other side. With everything we owned in our backpacks, I was sure we would sink. I kept worrying about things people had been doing for hundreds or thousands of years, and even though I knew it was ridiculous I couldn't stop the thoughts. This overthinking often plays out as negativity, so I tried to keep these thoughts from coming out of my mouth. We sat on the wooden plank bench and crossed without getting wet, though getting out of those low boats with a pack was a balancing act.

We only stayed in Laos a few days on our way to China, but we met two people who greatly impacted our entire overland journey. The first was Julie, a thin woman with a mane of red hair and silver bangles jingling on both arms. The Luang Namtha night market was in full swing, with vendors at booths selling food for immediate consumption. The night was warm, and we enjoyed a spicy papaya salad and people watching from the tables at the center. Julie walked by and asked if she could join us, and we immediately made room.

Julie was planning to take the bus the following morning to Vientiane, and we didn't envy her 10-hour journey on bumpy roads in what was probably a glorified minivan. We'd taken many similar journeys ourselves, mashed in with complete strangers and often holding someone's bag of onions or even a chicken. Julie was a bit older than most travelers we met, but her vivacious personality belied her true age. When she told us she was in her 70s we didn't believe her.

Julie spent her life traveling the world as an anthropologist along with her husband, and they enjoyed adventures in Asia, Africa, and beyond. She wrote books and lectured, and she found great reward in the way she lived her life. Since her husband wasn't with her we knew what was coming next. Since his recent death, she was continuing their travels and going to the places they loved. When we told her of our upcoming trip to Mongolia, she was mesmerized.

"I've always wanted to go there. You must tell me about it after you go." She scribbled out her email address on a piece of paper and handed it to me.

We were staying at the same hostel, and as we walked back she told us where we could rent bikes and suggested a route along the rice paddies. She gave me a dogeared book she'd just finished by Umberto Eco. This was a more highbrow read than my normal fare of thrillers and science fiction, and I was honored she thought I would like it. There were tables and chairs set out on the breezeways of our hostel, and we invited her to join us for tea before bed. She declined, saying she wanted to get in a session of yoga before bed so she'd be ready for her long bus ride the next day.

As we walked back to our room, we shook our heads at such a remarkable woman. Yoga at 10 p.m.? Traveling the world at 70-something, alone? Walking up to random strangers and making conversation? She reminded us of that couple we'd met in Barcelona so many years before. Julie was an incredible woman, and we couldn't help but wonder what we'd be like in our 70s. I'd like to think we'd still be traveling, meeting people, and adventuring, and healthy enough to bend our bodies in yogic positions, but if one of us were to die how would it impact our dreams? Would we be personally strong enough to continue, or was our partnership what propelled us forward?

It's hard to know the answers to these questions, but we appreciated she made us think of them. How long could we make this traveling lifestyle last? We knew there was no way we could see the entire world before we died, but how much could we see, and how long could we do this? And would we ever have to do it apart?

We were still talking about these questions on the bus into China the next day. We arrived in Jinghong, a bustling small city of about half a million people in the southern part of China. There were not a lot of Western people, and everywhere we went we got stares.

After a morning of visiting the Buddhist temple with a Chinese friend we made on the bus, we decided to stop for dumplings and found a shop near our hostel. The owner was a middle-aged woman in a smock apron. She was rolling out dough and stuffing them with meat as we took a seat at one of the plastic tables. Our new friend ordered for us and began chatting with the owner. He discovered she had just opened a few days before and was very excited to have Westerners in her shop. She took it as an omen of good fortune for her first business, and when we told her how much we loved dumplings she invited us back for a special dinner that night with her son.

We arrived to find a special table set outside the restaurant on the sidewalk for us. She brought out specialties from her home province in the Northeast of China, thousands of kilometers away.

We brought a bottle of rice wine as a gift, carefully selected from a vendor that afternoon, and we were gently told it was rubbish. She brought out the "good stuff" made by a local farmer, which she kept stashed in the back of the restaurant. We couldn't believe we were drinking Chinese moonshine. We learned how to toast the Northeast Chinese way (one by one and looking each other in the eye), and we drank to the shop owner's good fortune in business and the happy chance of getting to know each other.

Her son was studying to be a chef, and we talked about food and cultural similarities and differences between our two countries and even between their home province and Jinghong. After a couple of hours of eating and drinking, we learned the English translation of the restaurant name: Northeast Fat Mother Dumpling Shop. We nicknamed the owner our Little Dumpling, which made her laugh.

She wanted to know more about us, how to attract more travelers to her shop, and even how to talk to any Westerners she might see in the street. Her curiosity and enthusiasm kept us at her table well into the night, through a thunderstorm, and to the bottom of the bottle of rice wine.

Fat Mother said that night was one of her happiest in recent memory and we agreed with her, because China did not turn out to be a great destination for us. Our big expectations of walking into a country steeped in 5,000 years of history set us up for a very modern disappointment.

We stayed three months in this complex country, riding trains, buses and bicycles from the south to the north. We walked the Great Wall of China on a rare, smog-free sunny day. We hiked the trail at Tiger Leaping Gorge, one of the most beautiful walks in the world. We visited Tiananmen Square on the 23rd anniversary of the uprising, not surprised to see a greater military presence but otherwise no acknowledgment of the event with the heavily censored media of this country. We saw the famous Terra Cotta Warriors. We visited the Forbidden City, ate Peking duck, and tried unsuccessfully to master a few key phrases of Mandarin. We lived on noodle soup and pork buns for much of our time there because we didn't like anything else. The Chinese say that they'll eat anything with four legs that isn't a table, and they aren't joking. We dodged as much cigarette smoke as we could, along with the frequent spitting on the sidewalk and street.

Wow, the smoking and spitting and pissing and pooping. The density of people. The horrible smog and air quality. The strange and often inedible food. The people staring and snapping photos of our pale skin and big noses. ("Big nose" is actually a slang term for a foreigner.) After a while, our fascination with the history of China faded in light of the modern reality.

We attracted a lot of attention from people, especially in the southern parts of China, because we were so obviously different from them: taller, paler, with tattoos, and not part of a tour group. At first we liked it because people would engage with us, even if it was just to say "hello" and snap a picture. After a while, though, we didn't like the superficial interaction and the knowledge that we were just the "show and tell" item of the day. Cameras were shoved in our faces as we slurped our soup or sat on buses or even just walked down the street. We felt like Z-list celebrities on some bad reality television show. It was frustrating to always be on display, to always be the "other." We'd never felt that way anywhere before, even when we didn't look like the locals. We were learning what it was like to be a minority, and it wasn't comfortable.

The straw that broke the camel's back in our love affair with China was what we like to call the "new old." Everything in China was being modernized and expanded, and we could barely comprehend the scale of the megacities and public works projects like the Three Gorges Dam. Growth was explosive, and the burgeoning middle class demanded a more Western style of living. Malls, subways, highways, and bullet trains – everything we had in the West times ten was going on there. We called it Communist Capitalism. We couldn't blame people for wanting more luxury and convenience or for wanting to spend their growing disposable income on travel and material goods. What we found surprising, however, was the blatant disregard of the historical and natural assets of such an ancient civilization.

Ancient temples were rebuilt to look "new old," and quaint villages and towns were often completely razed and rebuilt to a conforming "new old" look filled with shops selling touristy souvenirs. The warren of alleys that made up the communal hutong neighborhoods in large cities like Beijing were being torn down and rebuilt with bars and restaurants to attract more tourists, while residents were shuffled into high-rise apartments. While not everyone was against this, there was no argument it changed the way of life of these people completely, going from a small community courtyard of co-living to isolated apartments.

Throughout these experiences we kept adjusting our expectations, putting a positive spin on things, and working overtime to make it okay. We felt guilty for not liking China after we'd spent so much time talking it up. We didn't want to admit defeat, but we simply didn't enjoy much of our time there and it was starting to weigh on our relationship.

In a normal situation we'd simply leave. But we'd turned our passports in to the Russian embassy to get our visas for the Trans-Mongolian Railway, so we couldn't leave until we got them back. And then we had expensive tickets to leave from Beijing to Russia, another consideration that kept us in place. We had to come up with a way to handle this uncomfortable situation in our remaining weeks there.

The first step was just to admit we didn't like it. For most of our relationship, I've been the Pollyanna to Warren's frustration. I always look for the bright side to make it less aggravating all around. This usually doesn't work because Warren wants to vent and get it over with, but I can't stop. It's my nature to look for the negative when things are positive and for the positive when things are negative. It's how I keep my mental balance.

But this time we had to be able to vent to each other. We didn't like it, and that was okay. We teamed up in our frustration, sharing the negativity together. Joking was a great relief at this point, from talking about being able to open the window and chew on the thick, smoggy air instead of going out for dinner to counting how many people would take our picture on any given outing. It helped ease the frustration to look at it sarcastically.

From that point, we changed our expectations to something more reasonable. We saw what we wanted to on our list, but we stopped trying to interact socially with people and make friends. We moved out of our hostel and into a small apartment in a residential area, writing, working, and cooking many of our own meals.

Culturally, we began to admire the modernity instead of condemn it. While there was no need to personally visit the high rises, dams, high-speed trains, and super highways being built at warp speed, we could appreciate the massive scale of these projects and the speed with which they were completed. We could use our VPN to access the "real" news from the outside world and then compare it to the message being shown inside China, a rare peek at the disconnect in real time.

We were in China during a time of intense cultural and economic change. We saw places that won't exist in five or ten years and witnessed the start of things that will dominate the country (and possibly the world) in the future. History was being made there, and it was awe-inspiring to watch it unfold.

We learned to admit when we weren't happy with a place, ignoring the guilt we had for not loving every destination in this lifestyle. We teamed up in our dissatisfaction instead of trying to talk each other out if it, fully immersing ourselves in the dislike of it all. By taking practical steps to ease our discomfort until we could leave, we didn't have to fake our way through it or give in to unhappiness. It was the best way we knew to make it through an unpleasant situation together.

By the time the Russian Embassy finally released our passports and visas, we were ready to leave China behind.

17

My Way or the Highway

Beijing's train station was mobbed. Short and slight people with farm clothes and giant sacks on their backs shared space with taller and fatter business travelers rolling designer luggage. These new arrivals from the countryside were wide-eyed at the city. No doubt this was the most people they had ever seen. How terrifying it must be to arrive in one of the most populated cities in the world direct from a rural farm and be expected to find a job.

Our transition to this life of travel had been difficult at times, but we always had the safety net of each other. We never had to go into a scary situation alone or feel the weight of our entire family's well-being on our shoulders. We were a team, and when we saw these overwhelmed farmers at the station we were reminded how lucky we were to be traveling through this life together.

Our next stop was Ulan Bator, Mongolia, two days away. We looked around the bustling train station as we made our way to the platform and realized this was the last major city we'd see until we reached Moscow in two months. After a lifetime of dreaming about it, watching movies, and reading books, we were finally boarding the Trans-Mongolian Railway, starting a journey by train across Mongolia and then continuing on the famous Trans-Siberian Railway across Russia. A few years before we met a couple in Seattle who'd done the journey themselves, and we were on the edge of our seats all evening as they recounted their trip. Now it was our turn to have these incredible experiences.

We boarded the train and found our second-class compartment, a room with two bunks on each side and a small table under the window in the middle. Our backpacks were stowed under the bottom bunk, and we sat our bag of food on the table.

As we pulled out of the Beijing train station and sped toward the desert of Mongolia, we watched the landscape change from the windows lining the hallway outside our compartment. Civilization gave way to rocky green hills, which then gave way to flat scrubland and then finally the desert. Eagles flew overhead, and as the train went around curves in the track we could see the length of it behind us snaking through the desert underneath a blue sky. In the distance we saw a herd of animals we thought were horses. How could they exist in such an inhospitable environment? As the train got closer, we realized they were camels, dozens of them.

We spent the next two days crossing the Gobi Desert, adjusting to the rhythm of the train chugging down the tracks into no man's land. The only people we saw after crossing into Mongolia were a father/child duo riding a dusty motorbike across the hard-packed dirt that eventually gave way to the desert. Finally we pulled into the train station at Ulan Bator, our home for the next several weeks. To the north were majestic mountains. To the south, inhospitable desert. We were at the oasis in the middle, ready for an adventure.

Buckets scattered the floor in the lobby as we walked into our guesthouse, catching the water as it dripped from the ceiling. It was rainy season, and the poorly constructed city of Ulan Bator was not faring well. Streets flooded, dirt alleyways were riddled with muddy holes, and sidewalks cracked from the shifting earth below. This was a stark difference from the rolling green hills and herds of wild horses we saw from our train window on the way in. But thinking about it made sense: what would a permanent city built by nomadic people look like? Ulan Bator, that's what.

But we weren't here to enjoy the city. We were here to see wild horses, to lay on our backs in the grassy steppes and watch eagles fly overhead. And to do that, we had to find a driver because Mongolia wasn't set up for the kind of independent travel we liked. Most of the roads weren't marked, or even officially roads. Getting around required a local and an SUV, and we were staying the night in Ulan Bator to find one.

Sancho came recommended by our hostel owner, who gave him a synopsis of the walking trip we wanted: 100 km (62 miles) through the steppes. Sancho agreed to a five-day trip with him supplying the gear if we brought our own food and water and paid for the gas. The negotiations were all done in Mongolian with our hostel owner, which should have alerted to us to one very big red flag.

As we drove out of Ulan Bator in the SUV toward the countryside, we soon realized Sancho spoke not a word of English. Not even hello. And our Mongolian was rustic, to say the least. We had a paper with some key phrases in Mongolian, including the standard greeting when approaching a nomadic family's ger camp: "Please hold your dog!"

We got worried. How would we handle the next five days in the wilds of Mongolia with a driver who spoke no English? We were antsy in the backseat, wondering how this little adventure was going to turn out. Why did we always have to do things the hard way? If we'd taken a tour with other people, this wouldn't have happened. But we couldn't deny that this challenge gave us a little thrill. We do things the hard way because that's what we like. This was just harder than usual.

As we bumped along the fields and makeshift roads toward the start of our walk, we decided to stop fretting and just let go. It would do us no good to worry until something bad actually happened, so our best bet to keep from ruining this experience would be to simply enjoy it as it unfolded. This was easier said than done, of course, especially when we realized there were only three million people in all of Mongolia, and half of those lived in Ulan Bator. Our chances of seeing more than a dozen people over the next five days were pretty small.

It was just us and Sancho, and we'd have to make do with what we had.

At our first stop, Sancho ushered us out of the SUV and then pointed in the direction we should go, through a valley with a small stream. He mimed meeting up with us later, and we set off wondering if we'd ever see him again. We had no idea where we were going, how long it would take to get there, and what the terrain would be like. It was the least control we'd ever had on a journey, and it freaked us out.

This feeling faded a bit as we walked across grassy plains toward clusters of trees, mooing at long-haired cows and bleating at sheep as we went past. Eagles soared overhead and horses grazed and ran in herds. There were no fences, posts, signs, or asphalt roads, and we slowly forgot our worries in such a peaceful and magical place. I thought back to the book I read, the story of Genghis Khan that first inspired our journey to Mongolia. I could see why Mongolians liked the freedom of living in felt gers for centuries, moving around this gorgeous land as they needed to in these big round tents.

Several kilometers later, we came upon Sancho parked in a field waiting to send us in a slightly different direction. We continued this way, meeting up with him every five kilometers or so to adjust our path. He directed us, showcasing the most beautiful parts of his country by pointing and grunting, and we simply followed along.

So much of our relationship, especially the business side, was tightly controlled. We made plans and deadlines, sorting out scenarios that would result in the most success. Everything for our small publishing business fell on our shoulders, and we weren't used to letting anyone else call the shots. Especially for Warren, the manager of our schedule and main planner of our travel, it was difficult to release control to someone else.

This discomfort at first made us testy with each other, feeling out of sorts and blaming the only other person who spoke English to vent our frustration. It took a while for us to realize what was going on, and if it weren't for the peaceful surroundings and hours of walking, we probably would have missed it.

Like facing our disappointment in China, we chose to band together instead of handling our discomfort alone. We began joking about this crazy situation we'd landed ourselves in, walking in the middle of Mongolia with a non-English-speaking driver we hoped would show up at the end of each day.

"Do you think today's the day we get stranded while Sancho drives off with our food and water?"

"Hey, do you think we'll get attacked by a marauding band of Mongols in our sleep tonight?"

"Those eagles keep circling overhead. Do you think they know something we don't?"

The jokes helped us make light of our situation and express our fears in a lighthearted way. Just getting them out in the open helped ease our stress as we gave ourselves up completely to a stranger's care.

The rest of the trip continued in the same vein, walking for half the day and stopping each afternoon at a beautiful spot, setting up camp, and enjoying a gorgeous sunset and a hot meal. On our last full day of hiking, we saw Sancho parked up on a hill much sooner than expected. It wasn't until we came to the peak that we saw the reason. In the distance was the 40-meter (131-foot) high metal statue of Genghis Khan astride his horse, one of the largest statues we have ever seen. And it was in the middle of nowhere.

We set up camp our last day in a field not far from the Genghis Khan statue. As we laid out our mats in the warm afternoon sunshine to read and relax, Sancho sat down beside us and tried to explain that he needed to leave. He motioned with his hands, much like you would to a dog, that we would stay. There were dark clouds developing in the distance and a storm on the way. Being alone in a tent on the open plain was not our idea of a good time.

"Stay, what do you mean, stay?" I was getting alarmed, and Warren put his hand on my arm to calm me down. It was hard to make a joke about being deserted in the face of a storm to fend for ourselves.

We had dozens of questions but no way to ask. He began cooking himself an early dinner, and we really got worried. How would he find our tent in the dark in this huge area? These Mongolians drove through fields all the time; more than likely he'd mow us down in our sleep.

Finally a van pulled up to our campsite and another driver plus an English-speaking man from our guesthouse emerged. He told us Sancho had to return early for a tour only he could do, so they were providing us with a new driver to take us home the following day. They moved all our belongings to the new van, introduced us to the new driver, and then took off with Sancho.

We were safe, had food to eat, and a dry place to sleep, just like all the other nights. We felt a little silly for having worried about it, still trying to exert control in a situation where we didn't have any. We made the mistake of thinking since it was our first time, it was everyone's first time.

I'm not sure we would have had this experience in letting go and living in the moment if we hadn't been forced into it. And without banding together to face the discomfort and even joke about it a little, we would have each spiraled out of control, missing out on what was the most beautiful country we'd ever seen.

When we gave up trying to manage all the details and get all the answers, bonding together in our discomfort instead of turning on each other, we had the time and space to let the wonders of Mongolia reveal herself to us.

18

Family Drama

Perched high up on a rock, we could see the trails of dust heading our way. After seeing less than 10 cars in the past four days, it was almost a traffic jam to watch a dozen heading across the desert straight for our ger camp.

We were in this remote location to witness a family reunion, Gobi Desert style. The owner of our hostel in Ulan Bator told us one of his employees wanted to go home to this reunion, and if we were interested we could hitch a ride and join the celebration. At first it felt weird to crash someone else's family fathering. Culturally, though, Mongolians were always a welcoming people; they just didn't often get the chance to do it because of the remote places they lived. We said yes to this once-in-a-lifetime opportunity.

Again, we'd be in a situation where no one spoke English, but we were growing more comfortable with giving up control, especially when the rewards were so great.

The matriarch of the family was 94 years old, a tiny woman who could be mistaken for a child at first glance, until she opened her mouth to make her wishes known. Her five children and their extended families were on their way to take part in honoring her, many of them from the "big city" of Ulan Bator. By 9 a.m. there were tents erected all around us, including two giant canopies to contain the food and the special seating area for the guests of honor. A lone goat was tied to a nearby rock, bleating at his fate.

In the center of one canopy was a giant blue barrel of airag, an alcoholic drink made from fermented mare's milk and vodka. It tasted like soured milk, and despite this it was a favorite drink of Mongolian men in the summertime, and had been for centuries. The women made huge batches of this drink for the reunion.

The celebration started at midday in the giant canopy with everyone gathering around. Most of the men and women had donned traditional Mongolian robes called deels, and the event took on a more reverent feel. We felt underdressed, Warren in his shorts and me in my khaki pants.

We tried to stay on the outskirts of the tent to give the family room to kneel in the shade, but we were ushered inside to take part in the festivities. As guests, we were almost as honored as the matriarch herself. Again, we realized they probably don't get a lot of visitors.

The matriarch started by giving blessings to the children with handfuls of candy. She included us in this ritual, and we ate our candy along with the kids, smearing chocolate on our hands in the desert heat.

After kneeling down, we were offered a large red plastic cup of airag. It would have been impolite to refuse, especially as everyone around us was downing it, so we bravely sipped ours. As our throats constricted and our eyes watered, we listened as family members stood to introduce their children and list their accomplishments to pay homage to the little mother who started it all. There were tears, laughter, and congratulations all around.

The drinks continued to flow, now including vodka and wine, and there were women wandering around dedicated to filling empty right hands. We discovered too late that the right hand was the drinking hand; empty ones will get a full cup of airag. Poor left-handed Warren learned this lesson the hard way when he got stuck with one in each hand.

The family then gave gifts to the matriarch. The presentation was beautiful, with brightly colored scarves serving as elaborate wrapping for each package. Our gift to her was a bottle of vodka, suggested by our hostel owner, which we thought she would add to the table of drinks for everyone. But she slipped it into her goodie bag of gifts next to her chair to save for later. Then she gave us more candy and a blessing.

As the sun continued to beat down, we began feeling the effects of the airag and vodka. It didn't take much in the dry desert air to bring on dehydration, and the sour taste made us a little nauseous. The first part of the celebration started winding down to allow people to rest in the heat of the day, so we found a shady spot in a cluster of rocks away from the camp to avoid another drink being placed in our hands.

Soon three boys joined us, and we spent the next hour teaching each other words in our respective language and singing songs from *The Lion King*. I don't know if I was more surprised to find out the boys knew the words to *The Lion King* song or that Warren did. I moved over to a shady rock a few feet away to observe Warren with the boys, snapping a few candid photos of them sweetly singing together. It was such a warm feeling watching him share this song and laughing with the boys.

If we had chosen to have children, he would have been a terrific father. Even now, he's great with kids in the limited situations in which we see them. I remembered what I considered the magical age of my nieces and nephew: seven. It was the time they were old enough to carry on a conversation, excited to learn more about the world, and still thought adults were cool. Now they were adults themselves. As the matriarch of the family in the Gobi Desert was presiding over the reunion, I realized we would never have this kind of experience since we chose not to have children. It was a strange thought, one that didn't cause any anxiety or regret; simply a statement on what could and could not be. Years earlier I'd had my tubes tied, and from our very first conversation we were in sync on the decision to not have children.

Over the years we've caught some heat for this decision, as if other people have a vote in the matter. Acquaintances and strangers both have told us that having children is "the next step," whatever that means. But throughout the ups and downs of life, finding our way individually and as a couple, this has never been a question for us, never been an issue. But for other people it is.

And that's always been our issue. We know how we feel about it for ourselves, and we made a decision that suits us. But in much of the world having children is a rite of passage, the event that signals adulthood. Marriage is as much an economic and social institution as it is for love, and people in other countries often don't understand why we're married if we don't have children.

We haven't spent a lot of time examining our decision because it just felt right for us, but we've had plenty of time to examine other people's opinion of our decision because it keeps coming up. When they see us play with children there must be a secret longing. When we choose to avoid children, we must be child-haters. There is a lot of meaning given to a decision we never think about ourselves, and we find this strange. We joke about going around asking these same people why they chose to have children, forcing them to justify their decision in the same way they want us to. But frankly, we don't care. Everyone should be free to make their own family planning decisions without the input from strangers. We gently refused the services of the Mongolian man who wanted to show us just how you impregnate a woman, as if ignorance was the reason we didn't have children yet.

After our sing-along with the boys, people woke from their naps and the goat was brought out. It had been cooked with hot stones sewn up inside its belly in the traditional Mongolian way. By this time, several of the men were staggering more than walking and many of the younger people had changed out of deels and back into their summer clothes, which gave Warren the opportunity to try one on. After they dressed him in a dark green robe with an orange sash, the Mongolian men patted him on the back and pointed at the flip-flops on his feet and the beard on his face. He had a ways to go to look like a stone-faced Mongolian horseman.

That evening as the sun went down the music started. All day solar panels charged so songs could be played throughout the night. The Mongolian DJ played Adele and Jason Mraz and even some Michael Jackson. As the night wore on, the music turned traditional, long songs about life, love and loss from famous Mongolian singers. Near midnight, the music stopped and everyone joined together to sing a cappella under a blanket of stars. We couldn't believe we were there to experience such a beautiful moment. We went to sleep in our ger that night to the sounds of old women singing the songs of their ancestors in the silent desert, peering at the stars through the top vent, and feeling like the luckiest people on earth to witness the gathering of this clan.

Our own clan is more hodge-podge, made up of friends and family around the world. We'll probably never gather at one place to honor us or any other member specifically, and our songs are all different. But everywhere we go we add a new member to our clan, making the entire world the setting for our family reunion. Our sisters and brothers and cousins and aunts and uncles are made up of the people who've chosen to be part of our family, and we're honored to be included in theirs.

We don't look alike. We don't act alike. And we're not even of the same race or age or socioeconomic status. But we're family.

Everyone makes choices in life, and as we go through our 40s we feel the result of all the decisions we've made to this point. And we're happy with them. The life we live may not be right for everyone, and that's okay. It's right for us, and that's all that counts.

19

Getting a Lock on Love

The bridges in Russia were covered in padlocks of all shapes and sizes. Hundreds if not thousands adorned every bridge we crossed, all carved with initials and dates. Since we don't read Cyrillic, we had to ask. What was this?

The locks were a romantic tradition in Russia and beyond, in which couples carve their names on a lock, attach it to a bridge, and then throw the key into the water. It means their love will last forever, or at least until the lock falls off the bridge. We saw these lock-covered bridges throughout our journey on the Trans-Siberian Railway on every stop from Siberia to St. Petersburg. It was beautiful to see reminders of love all over a very functional piece of everyday life. We imagined it would feel special to pass by on foot and touch your own lock or be reminded of the day you attached it every time you took the train to work.

Everyday reminders of love and commitment are important in keeping a relationship strong.

It wasn't just the locks, though. Russia was nothing like what we thought it would be. In Siberia, the sturdy wooden houses were decorated with bright shutters and doors. Fields of purple and yellow flowers, a gorgeous blur of color fronted the long expanses of birch forest as our train sped by. Women wore colorful scarves, from the elderly babushkas all the way down to young girls. With such a long winter to cope with, these people proclaimed their love and hope of the eventual spring with as much color as they could find.

This was all so different from what we expected of our former Cold War adversaries. Warren and I both graduated from high school in 1989, the end of the arms race, the fall of the Berlin Wall, the breakup of the Soviet Union, and the supposed downfall of communism. We were expecting drab, dour people, concrete block buildings, and lots of smoking and despair a la Dostoevsky. Just like we had in China, we let our expectations color our experience unfairly. But unlike China, our experience in Russia was even better than we hoped.

Some of the stereotypes were true, of course. We observed drinking as a huge problem in Russia, and it was not unusual to see drunk men at any hour of the day. But aside from the more-than-occasional public drunkenness, Russia was fascinating. Over five days of train travel Russia revealed herself to us, a colorful contrast to what we expected. The Trans-Siberian Railway gave us a window into the history and culture of Russia as we sped along the tracks. The wooden houses of Siberia gave way to the one-of-a-kind St. Basil's Cathedral in the Red Square of Moscow which gave way to the distinctly European look of St.

Petersburg. It was here, in this ornate city on the Neva River founded by Peter the Great, that we first saw a Russian wedding – one of many.

The first bride and groom we saw bounded down the steps of the church and into the street as the wedding photographer caught them mid stride. We stopped to watch the couple in their wedding-day finery, snapped a few of our own photos, and considered the Russian attitude toward love.

A limousine was waiting to take them around St. Petersburg to pose for photographs. The tradition for a wedding was to go to a church (if religious), followed by a civil ceremony to make it legal, then cake and drinks with friends followed by a limo tour of the historic monuments with a photographer. We were there on a sunny weekend in the summer, so we saw at least a dozen couples being photographed next to statues honoring Peter the Great, Catherine the Great, and even Dostoevsky, who was apparently not great enough to garner a Great after his name. Couples spent hours after their weddings being chauffeured around to all the historic sites they'd likely passed a thousand times in their lives. Having a photo next to one sent the message: "Our love is here to stay, just like this chunk of marble."

Far from being the stoic, practical types we expected, Russians were love crazy. These weren't dry "comrade-to-comrade" unions. They proclaimed their affections with locks on bridges, elaborate wedding outfits, fancy chauffeurs in outrageous cars, and pictures at all the permanent monuments in the city. These actions proclaimed to everyone they were in love and meant it to last.

But this only worked for heterosexual couples. At the same time we were watching couples celebrate their love, new friends we met on the Trans-Siberian Railway could have none of it. They were two gay men from the U.S., and even though they were traveling together as friends, neither could venture out to the gay bars and clubs of Russia without worry of reprisals. Cops were raiding clubs, including the only lesbian bar we saw in all of Russia, and punishing people for who they chose to love. Love and the appreciation of love was reserved for heterosexual couples only.

We spoke with one of the men who decided to go out anyway, leaving his more cautious friend at the hotel. He told us of the types of men he met at these clubs, men with both powerful jobs and lowly positions, men from every walk of life. They all had established lives in Russia, but they couldn't do the one thing they most wanted: have a public relationship.

Whatever problems we've had in the past, we've never had a public denouncement of our love or outside forces to contend with. When we looked at our life and love through that lens, it made all our problems shrink in comparison. We might fight it out over family or money or sex or power, but we've never had to fight outside forces to simply exist. We never had to deal with problems from outsiders before we dealt with our internal problems.

Love was complicated enough, and we couldn't imagine the extra pressure gay couples had to endure. Why couldn't they be as loud and proud as we were?

Why couldn't they have locks on bridges, weddings in courthouses, and pictures with monuments?

This was a longstanding argument of ours, that we were no different from any committed gay couple. We didn't want children. At that point we couldn't even have children, thanks to a tubal ligation. Our only purpose was to be together. We gladly paid our taxes for roads, schools, hospitals, firefighters, policemen, and everything else that made a society run. In return, we got certain legal protections and tax breaks for being legally married. So if we could have a government-sanctioned relationship, why couldn't our gay friends?

We have an inordinately large number of gay friends. It's not because we seek them out; it's because we lead similar lifestyles and naturally seem to find each other. The experts say that up to 10% of the population is gay. More than 10% of the travelers we meet are gay. More than 10% of the entrepreneurs we meet are gay. More than 10% of our close friends are gay. We run in unconventional circles that attract outliers, and we are privileged to see their perspective and witness their lives. And frankly, they aren't that dissimilar from our own.

The locks on the bridge showed commitment made by humans to other humans. It didn't mean that all heterosexuals were faithful, that all Russians were heterosexual, or even that love always lasted. What it meant was that in that moment, for the future that couple imagined, they were together. And they hoped it stayed that way.

What more could someone hope for in this life than a commitment to be true to each other? A public declaration of love and an expectation of acceptance and even congratulations from their fellow humans? We're used to having it, to seeing images in the media and movies that confirm our way of loving. Imagine being on the outside, unable to take those photos, to see love like yours displayed in movies, to hold hands in public, or even live together openly? As much as we appreciated the love we saw in Russia, we were also privy to the love you couldn't see in Russia. Two years later, as the Olympics in Sochi were underway, we weren't surprised to see the homophobic response from the Russian government. Once again, we were reminded of our Western, heterosexual privilege in the world. We felt extremely lucky and extremely guilty.

There are many things to be embarrassed about in our relationship. I routinely forget the punchline or most important point to every story. Warren will debate anyone on just about any topic for the sake of the argument. We are both too loud, talk too much, and given enough hours and access we have a tendency to go heavy on the wine. We're bossy and tend to try to control the group itinerary. We are a tad bit cheap. And we probably use too much profanity.

But we never have to be embarrassed about our relationship, to explain it or rationalize it or hide it. And this means our problems are all within our control to fix; they are all created by us. We can change our words, our spending, our habits, and our attitudes. But we can't change those of others, and we mourn for those in Russia and everywhere else who can't openly work on their relationships like we do. They can put a lock on a bridge, but they can't hold hands in the street. And that makes our problems pale in comparison.

Because we can be proud of our love, we will. We'll be schmoopy and schmaltzy and kiss and hold hands and laugh out loud at our private jokes in public. And we'll do everything within our own environment to make it safe for others to do the same.

'Til the bridge comes tumbling down.

20

The Great Understanding

The clerk couldn't understand a word we were saying. Our German was poor, and in Austria it was unintelligible. We were trying to order lunch at a brewery just over the border from Slovenia. We were staying at a farmhouse in Slovenia with some American friends we met the previous winter in Thailand, Russ and Michelle. They were booked all summer house sitting in the countryside of Slovenia. This day trip into Austria together was simply to walk among the vineyards and get a little exercise. Unfortunately, the day turned out to be too hot for that idea, so we switched to plan B, visiting a local brewery.

Just when we were about to give up on our order, a dark-haired woman behind us stepped up to help. Her name was Lydia, and she was buying a few growlers of specialty beer as a gift for her husband, who was coming home that weekend after a work trip. For sorting out our troubles, we invited her to join us for lunch.

Lydia and her husband had recently renovated a house in the countryside with a small vineyard, which they leased out to a winery. She worked from home doing translations, and her husband flew to Paris every week for work, returning to their little slice of paradise on weekends. She had an exotic, international look and cosmopolitan style, like Christiane Amanpour. Lydia was the over-40 package every woman wants to be: confident, accomplished, and sure of her continued sex appeal.

It was a gorgeous, sunny day, and one beer with Lydia stretched into two. Then the lead brewer came out to give a demonstration on harvesting hops, which we all went out to watch. A small group of people joined us, including one older man who claimed he was in the Austrian army with Arnold Schwarzenegger in his youth. We asked him what he was like. "Silly man, always joking" was his opinion of the former governor of California.

After the demonstration, Lydia invited us all to come back to her house. She said it was a shame to come into Austria and not get to sample the region's wine, and her home had a stocked cellar of the wine produced from her grapes. The short drive to her house was beautiful, and we could easily see why they chose to live there. And like every traveler we've met, she was at ease meeting new people and making friendships. We sat in the yard of her beautiful home, curled up in giant wooden chairs, slowly sipping wine made from her grapes and talking about life, love, travel, and friends. It was an easy conversation that lasted into the fading light of the day, the sun going down behind the vineyard on the side of the house.

Before leaving, we went down into the basement of the barn, which was converted into a cellar for wine. She pulled a bottle of her namesake red wine, Lydia, from the rack and gave it to us to commemorate the day. On the way back to the farmhouse, we decided to save it for a special dinner together before we left.

A few days later Michelle and I were sitting at the kitchen table, sorting through the recent pickings from the farm's vegetable garden. It was a cozy kind of afternoon you have with comfortable friends. I didn't often get to spend time with girlfriends like this, so I treasured every moment. We talked about books, politics, body image, and aging, among other things. Those "after 40" revelations of finally getting to know ourselves and feeling more comfortable in our skin were coming out, and I was beginning to think this farmhouse was a magical place. It was like one of those Hallmark movie moments, two women sitting in a farmhouse kitchen drinking tea and revealing themselves to one another. In the past I would have made fun of such a cliché, but in the moment, it made my heart soar.

I told Michelle about a recent discovery that explained a lot of the trouble I had in the past fitting into the world, especially in this lifestyle of travel and meeting new people all the time. It wasn't that I was socially awkward or didn't like to be around people. There was finally a label for being adept at social situations but only wanting so much of them - I was an introvert.

I told her I'd learned that introversion was the not the same thing as shyness, and how I gained energy from being alone and drained energy around other people (one of the tell-tale traits of introverts). Me in a social situation was like watching the battery signal go down on a laptop or cell phone. I performed very well for a set period of time, but when I was done, I was done. I couldn't do any more, and I needed to retreat to recharge. Michelle was also an introvert, and we had a lively discussion about the tricks and tools we've used over the years to make us function in what seemed like an extroverted world.

I didn't pay any attention to Warren and Russ, who were off doing their own thing. Occasionally they would wander into the kitchen to get a glass of water or ask about the vegetables we just picked, but mostly they kept to themselves. It was a beautiful day, and we marveled at how lucky we were to spend this time together in a farmhouse in this scenic part of the world. I'm embarrassed to admit this, but before they invited us to join them, I didn't even know where Slovenia was. And now it was the location of one of the sweetest and most mature conversations I'd ever had with a friend about being a woman.

Later that night as we were getting ready for bed, Warren told me he overheard our conversation. We weren't talking about anything private or anything I wouldn't have said to him, so I didn't understand why he was bringing it up. He said overhearing my statement about being an introvert was like fireworks going off in his head. Learning that I gained my energy internally gave him more understanding of me than he'd had in years (and he was no slouch in the understanding department). While he always knew I "hit the wall" at a certain point socially, he never understood why before that night. This explained why I distanced myself from him and needed so much time alone. For the first time, he realized it had nothing to do with him. It was a lightbulb moment in our relationship.

I've told Warren a million times that I need time to process, think things through, or be alone, but it wasn't until he understood that I gained energy from being alone so I can be with people later that it became clear why. I kept calling myself an introvert, but I never defined it for him and he never asked for a definition. We both thought we understood, but we didn't.

He was relieved to find out that I don't retreat to read or nap because I want to get away from him; I do it to recharge and come back for more. I don't leave the party early because I'm antisocial; I do it because I'm at my limit of energy. I don't have a problem with shyness or an inability to speak up; I simply don't want to spend all day speaking with other people.

I was surprised that Warren didn't know this about me, and he was surprised I hadn't spelled it out sooner. All those times he took my distance as a personal attack were simply me recharging to come back for more interaction. I couldn't understand why he pushed for interaction sometimes when he knew I didn't want it, or why he wouldn't give me the space I needed, the space I specifically asked for. He felt rejected because he didn't know the reason and wanted to reconnect. He wanted to know we were okay because my actions told him we weren't. And it took almost 10 years together and a trip to Slovenia to finally figure out where we were coming from.

As we laid in bed, we talked through some of the situations we'd been in recently. I explained how I felt throughout – why the situation with Lydia at the brewery was so enjoyable because it was a small group, and why going to large parties was a nightmare. It was why I loved our time in Slovenia but hated the idea of going to Munich next for Oktoberfest.

Of course, being an introvert didn't mean I got to have things my way all the time. Warren loved being around other people, and he regularly started conversations with strangers on the street, something I'd never do unless I was asking for directions. He wanted to go to parties, meet new people, and tell stories late into the night. He never wanted to do anything alone, sharing every experience with me and then talking about it when it was over. What exhausted me energized him, and what filled me up bored him to tears.

He loved the family reunion in the Gobi Desert, making the effort to communicate with dozens of people through a language barrier for hours upon hours. There were moments I had to escape to the ger for a moment of peace and quiet. On the Trans-Mongolian train from Beijing to Ulan Bator, he talked up every single person in our car while I happily read my book and chatted only with the two teachers in our compartment. On the cruise to Antarctica, Warren made friends with virtually all 120 people on the cruise. I selected only a handful to get to know.

Looking at the evidence, it was easy to see the trends. But because we'd not specifically looked at it this way before, it just didn't click. But now it did, and we wanted to find a way to be better in sync with each other. As we talked it out, we came to realize that we don't have to bend and sway to be like each other. We simply have to give each other space to be who we are.

When that happens, we bring the best of ourselves to the relationship.

If I'm tired, I'll leave the party early and there are no hard feelings. He can stay and enjoy the fun. If we've been alone for too long, I need to make the effort to go out with him and be around other people. He gives me time alone before or after to recharge. It sounds so simple, but in the past we didn't appreciate our differences, taking the other's behavior as a snub or an aggravation. For the first time, we realized the other's behavior was all about them and we should take our egos out of the equation. We agreed then to let each other blossom in the way that worked best, no longer applying pressure to conform, and giving each other as much of what we needed as we could.

A few nights later we sat around the farmhouse table to share that bottle of Lydia wine with a meal cooked from the overflowing farmhouse garden, toasting our friendship, new discoveries about each other, and how a relationship was a constantly evolving thing. Warren and Russ stayed up talking late into the night, and the two introverts left early to read. As it should be.

Part III: SMOOTH(ER) SAILING

21

The Love Contract

The sun was rising over the hill across the valley, and we'd just spent an hour walking up in the twilight. Warren conceived of this romantic adventure as a way to celebrate our ninth anniversary, and I was none too pleased about it. We were in central Mexico, and the walk was more of a climb than a saunter. The trail went over rocks, sliding shale, and steep hills, requiring us to scramble in the dark with our headlamps. This anniversary was the least romantic in memory.

We set out in the dark, climbing first up a narrow road to get to the trail. Cars occasionally whizzed by, and I could hear a herd of goats ahead. Even with a headlamp, I could hardly see anything and I was getting frustrated at being woken up so early to climb in the dangerous dark to a hill we'd been on a dozen times already. This was not my idea of romance, but I had foolishly agreed to it the day before.

Warren was fed up with my attitude, and I told him there was no reason we had to climb in the dark. It was dangerous and stupid. He was mad because I was spoiling the plans we'd already agreed to do. We stopped along the way and got into a fight as the herd of goats passed by. If we hadn't been so mad at each other we probably would have laughed. Warren urged us on so we could get to the top before sunrise. I trudged along behind him, cursing, and he used his anger to propel himself forward faster. This meant he took his light with him, so I had even less than before. There was no teamwork that morning.

We finally arrived at the top, and the sun was still behind the hills on the other side of the valley. I was pissed, realizing we got there about 30 minutes too early. Had we left later we would have had a bit more sleep, a bit more light, and probably less fighting – at least that was my logic. We took seats on the boulders and faced the direction of the sunrise, silently seething at each other. Neither one of us were feeling romantic.

Warren turned to me and asked, "Do you want to stay married?"

It sounds harsh, but it was an agreed-upon anniversary conversation. Despite the rough start to our day, we did have important business to discuss. I gathered my thoughts as we watched the light grow, thinking back to when we first contractualized our relationship into one-year agreements.

For us it started with the novel *Cutting for Stone* by Abraham Verghese. One of the couples in the book has a similar story to ours, at least in terms of the merging and clashing of personalities.

In the book, when Ghosh asked Hema to marry him, she surprised him by saying yes, but only for a year. He was stunned, telling her he wanted to be with her forever and ever. She replied that he might be sure, but she wasn't. So why not try it for a year with an option to renew?

The first time I read the passage I thought it was brilliant. Then I thought it through and compared it to our relationship, and I wondered what Warren would say. We were pretty fresh from our big relationship awakening in Massachusetts and newly settled in Seattle. Things were good, but what would he say if I asked the question?

Hema and Ghosh were supporting characters to the story, but I was drawn to their complex relationship and the nontraditional way they made it work. At least in the personality department, we had a lot in common. I brought up the subject over dinner, telling Warren about the book and the beautiful story within. I read the passage about the one-year marriage out loud, wondering what he'd say.

His logical brain immediately leapt at the idea, an annual conversation to discuss what was going well, what needed improvement, and what the immediate future looked like. He liked the concept of an annual contract negotiation, putting our relationship into the context of business and the never-ending quest to be more profitable. In this case, the balance sheet measured love and happiness. One thing Warren didn't like, though, was the ability to call it quits. He wanted to remain committed to each other no matter what. As a serial monogamist, he thought the "easy out" would keep us from working on any big problems.

The more I thought about it, the more I liked the out. It gave a true urgency to the negotiation, because if we knew we'd stay together no matter what, it would make the difficult conversations less likely to happen. The out was what made this concept work, the idea that one of us could call it quits if things got too bad. It was the incentive we needed to not let our relationship deteriorate to that level. It was a risk, but the risk is what made the reward so great.

We decided to give it a try, pledging that day to stay married until our next anniversary, on April 23, and then renegotiate. We weren't sweeping our problems under the rug for a year, but we were pledging to address negative trends and voice our future desires in a formal way every year and get an official commitment to make our relationship stronger.

While on the surface this sounds harsh, in reality it is quite romantic. We choose each and every year to stay together, and we also use this time to discuss what's going really well and what we'd like to see change. This active management of our relationship has allowed us to say difficult things to each other with love and an open mind and to make incredible changes that might otherwise be impossible to suggest, much less carry out.

One year Warren told me I was gaining too much weight. This was the kind of statement that couldn't easily come up in day-to-day conversation. With my brother's early heart attack, my weight gain was more than just aesthetics, though knowing he found me less attractive was hard to take. He told me both for the physical part of our relationship and because he wanted me around until our old age. Without an annual review, I doubt this complaint would have ever reached the light of day, at least not in the way that resulted in a positive change in my health or our relationship. Since that conversation, I lost 50 pounds and felt and looked better than I had in years.

On one anniversary I told Warren his personal habits were a turn-off. He was becoming more casual in our relationship, and his comfort with doing private things in front of me made me less inclined to want him physically. He was surprised to hear this, thinking the comfort together was a good thing. But when he realized activities like scratching himself in front of me meant less sex, he was motivated to change. And then we had more sex.

We don't start with the fat ass or ball scratching in these negotiations, of course. We start with the positive, the things that are going well in our relationship. Congratulations and appreciation abound for what is good and should be continued. It sets us up for the more difficult conversation to follow, because no one wants to be the bearer or the recipient of bad news. But if not now, when? How long do you let a relationship slide before you step in?

We began calling our annual review the Love Contract. It's not a formal statement or document, but it does go through a formal review process. And this uncomfortable conversation has given us the greatest odds of reaching our golden anniversary.

The first year we traveled, we had our annual love contract negotiation on a ship crossing the Atlantic. We were able to eat a nice meal, look out over the sea, and proclaim our love and commitment to each other under the stars. The next year we were in China and spent the afternoon on the deserted rooftop of an Irish bar, drinking Tsingtao beer and sharing the excitement of our first days in that complex country. This year we'll have our negotiation in Spain with plenty of sunshine, tapas, and wine.

The surroundings have an effect on our negotiation, but just barely. No matter where we are, the goal is to focus on our relationship and where we're failing and where we're succeeding.

It's an option we give each other on every anniversary, making our love a true partnership where the contract is up for negotiation. Saying "I do" is something we do on an annual basis to make sure we don't wake up one day wondering what the hell went wrong with our relationship.

When we first started doing this in 2006, it was an iffy time. We were slowly rebuilding our trust, but the agreement to work on our relationship together solidified the commitment. By the time our renewal came around a year later, we were back on track.

Like many couples, we had the security and responsibility of a house and bills to tie us together. But as we got rid of everything we owned and began traveling in 2010, there were no possessions or commitments to tie us together. If we wanted to go our separate ways, it would be almost as easy as breaking up was in high school. There was nothing to split but money, no house or china or kids to fight over. Nothing kept us together except our commitment.

"Happily ever after" doesn't exist without work, which is why we've always resisted the idea of the wedding day as the happiest of our lives. Shouldn't it just be the start of a happiness that grows over time?

Back on the boulder in Mexico, we were both calming down and approaching the negotiation with more care than we did our path to get there. After a few minutes of measured breathing to regain our composure, we started our negotiations.

"So what do you like about the way our relationship worked this past year?" I asked. As he began listing our accomplishments as a team, both in business and personally, the mood softened. I moved closer to him on the rock.

Then I listed the ways I loved our relationship and what I thought worked for us. He softened a bit as I outlined our good points. Despite the fight on the way up, we were starting to warm to the topic at hand. By the time we got to the problems, we were ready to discuss them rationally and focus on solutions. I couldn't believe the angry people we were at the start of the conversation were the mature people who boosted the power of their relationship at the end.

Over the years this process has given us a sounding board to encourage good trends and reverse bad ones. But it's also made us more comfortable sharing our feelings on a day-to-day basis. We don't have to wait a year to complain about something. The forum is more to address trends that don't have a specific moment. But ironically, it has helped us address more of the trends that do have a specific trigger, calling out problems in a way that encourages solution and reduces the hurt. It's never going to be ideal to tell each other we're not measuring up, either in the day to day or in the annual review, but it's far better than waiting until we are too far gone to fix.

As we finished our negotiation, the sun rose over the mountain across the valley. We looked at each other and asked if we wanted to make a go of it for another year. Without pause, we both said yes.

Then we climbed down the mountain together in the sunshine.

22

Disconnect to Reconnect

People are usually surprised to discover we haven't owned a cell phone since 2010. When we make plans with people, we just show up at the agreed-upon time. There are no "on my way!" or "running late!" or "sorry, can't make it" texts from us. What freaks other people out is that they can't send those same messages to us. When we make plans we follow through, and people are compelled to show up or be the rude no-shows because they can't reach us. These days it's just too easy for people to bail out, and they aren't used to being held to plans they made days or weeks before.

We once made plans to meet up with a friend at the port in Miami at a certain date and time. We left Copenhagen on a ship and spent two weeks crossing the sea with no internet access in between. When we got off the boat, we found her just like we planned. She couldn't believe we didn't have a phone to coordinate our meet up and just trusted she'd find us. Some people consider us rebels, as if our old-school approach to communication is cowboy cool. Not everyone can live without a phone, but we can and choose to do.

Far from being Luddites, we actually make our living online so we get plenty of time in front of the screen; it just happens to be laptops instead of phones. We've come a long way from our overworked, overconnected days, and despite our website, podcast, and books, we do like to spend most of our time offline. We never wanted to go back to those days of being connected to everyone else but each other.

In these moments away from people, updates, news, gossip, and cat videos, we find ourselves, both individually and as a couple. If we go too long living indoors without a sabbatical from the busyness of life, we go a little stir crazy. It affects our mental health and our relationship in a negative way.

In the summer of 2013 we spent a month in the north of England, house- and pet-sitting for a small menagerie of animals in a quaint farmhouse. There were dogs, chickens, doves, hamsters, and a cat. There was only one small shop in town for groceries as well as one pub, the community meeting place. As we nestled into this bucolic life, we could feel ourselves getting closer to each other. Without the hustle and bustle of the outside world, we were reconnecting to our inner world. It was simple and easy.

When the house sit ended, we decided to go deeper and take our tents and backpacks to Scotland, where we'd walk the 94 miles of the West Highland Way together, wild camping along the way. There would be no Facebook, no news, and no appointments. Just us and Mother Nature, alone for a week.

We strapped on our backpacks and set off walking, not expecting any withdrawal pains from the world. But old habits die hard. At first, we manually Googled each other with questions we'd normally look up online.

"How far do you think it is until the next town?"

"What's the weather forecast for tomorrow?"

"How do you pitch a tent in the wind?"

There was no Wikipedia, no Weather Channel, and no guru to guide us on these vital questions. We simply had to figure them out ourselves, starting conversations about things we'd been managing digitally for years.

We started watching the sky for signs of changing weather, or asking locals as we passed through villages how far to the next one. It felt revolutionary to be so primitive. *Look at us; we're watching the sky!*

Over time our conversations shifted. We went from short, choppy talks with a definite purpose to more meandering discussions that ended up in surprising places.

In the evenings, we pitched our tent in the green forested areas, soaking our tired feet in the cool water of a nearby stream or lake and preparing simple dinners. Warren wandered with his camera, snapping photos of mushrooms, exotic flowers, and Highland cows. I wrote in my notebook and daydreamed. Sometimes we played cards in the tent before bed.

The third day, we arrived at a rustic cafe at the gorgeous Scottish lake called Loch Lomond. We set down our heavy packs and ordered coffee and a bacon butty, which is a hearty bacon sandwich perfect for calorie-deprived backpackers. As we were finishing our breakfast at the picnic table outside, two older women stopped by to ask if we were walking the West Highland Way. They asked where we were from and what we did for a living, to which Warren explained we were American writers who traveled. When they asked what kind of books we wrote, Warren jokingly told them "erotica," expecting to shock them a little. One woman didn't miss a bit, immediately taking a seat at the picnic table and leaning forward, chin resting on her hand.

"Do tell!" she said.

After sharing a fun laugh and fond farewells, we strapped on our packs and began walking again. It wasn't long before Warren said,

"You know, we could write an erotic novel."

We then spent hours mapping out the characters and plot points of a travel-based erotic novel. We huffed and puffed and grunted our way through a rocky climb while discussing the finer points of seduction in locations around the world.

These types of conversations were hard to have in everyday life because of interruptions. But out on the trail, we imagined our main character's entire story, tested out alternate endings, and surprised each other with our take on what erotica really was. We even came up with a pen name to hide our identities.

Sometimes we spent hours in solitude, thinking our own thoughts. It wasn't always deep thinking, either. I remember spending a great deal of time one day wondering if my life would be easier if I grew my hair out and whether it was too late to really appreciate the benefits of Lasik eye surgery now that I had to wear reading glasses.

Increased focus was the change we noticed the most during the our time away. Our interests and thoughts remained generally the same, but the level of focus increased exponentially. We could think about haircuts, erotic novels, travel, relationships, books, and food with more attention and focus than ever before.

There were no interruptions or distractions, and our conversations were funnier, more intense, and generally more satisfying. (Or maybe that's because we were mentally writing an erotic novel.) We both spent time in the evenings scribbling in our notebooks in the tent, capturing the ideas from the day. One day maybe we'll write that erotic novel.

Warren expected to find great insights during his time offline, a flood of ideas to fill his head once he turned off his email. That didn't happen. At first he was disappointed, thinking our retreat wasn't working. But we talked about it and realized that sometimes you just need to clear things out so something new can come in later. He stopped feeling bad about it and just focused on enjoying the experience.

On the sixth night, we stayed in a hostel. When we arrived, we took the most satisfying shower in the world, enjoyed a hot meal, and took a nap. When woke up later, we decided to make hot chocolate in the common room. The TV was on, immediately killing the zen we had from our tech-less journey. We made our hot chocolate and immediately went back to the serenity of our room.

As the trek wound down and we finally began our descent into Fort William, a quaint village at the foot of the mighty Ben Nevis, the U.K.'s tallest mountain, we were feeling pretty good.

We went eight days without the internet and the outside world and survived. We mentally wrote a book. We gave our full attention to each other. Our entire experience was alone, without any likes or shares or comments from anyone else. We had no polls or quizzes or cat videos to distract us. The celebrities did their thing without our attention, and news came and went without our knowledge. All conversations with the outside world were put on hold. It taught us that we can escape the world for a while and reconnect with each other without any lasting harm. The internet still functions even when we're not using it, and we can drop in and out as much as it fits our lifestyle. Technology is available all the time, but we don't have to be. And when we can give our full attention to each other, it recharges our relationship more than anything we can get from the outside world.

23

Living In Crazy Town

I was writing in the alcove off our bedroom in Mexico when I heard yelling...in English. Normally I could hear drifts of Spanish conversation and music in the breezy desert air, but never English in this artsy Mexican town. And never my husband yelling at the top of his lungs.

At this point we were about two months into our winter stay in the hills of central Mexico, and we were already well into our third year of travel. The weather and people were ideal, but our living arrangements were not. Warren booked this three-bedroom house online after an email exchange with the American owner, and it was rustic to say the least. The first few mornings we woke up to a dozen snails in our kitchen due to a water leak under the sink.

The landlord was a grumpy old man who guarded his last peso. He wanted top rates for his rentals, but he didn't want to invest in them. We were of the opinion that a daily snail infestation and regular kitchen flooding was probably something that needed to be addressed. After several days, he begrudgingly agreed. His house was in the same compound as our rental property, and we all lived behind a gate.

Over the weeks the landlord's negative manner and constant fear of being cheated began to wear on us. If we happened to get trapped by him near the gate as we were leaving, he'd tell us how he swindled someone out of money in the past or how someone tried to rip him off, sometimes for the equivalent of a dollar. He became our symbol for everything we didn't want to be as we got older, and his isolation and drinking appeared to be heavy contributors to his unhappiness.

Normally we wouldn't stay in such a negative situation, but it was high season and friends had already booked flights to come see us. To move to another house of equivalent size would break our budget, so we decided to stick it out and just avoid him as much as possible.

Our various friends arrived throughout those two months and stayed from a few days to a couple of weeks at a time. We wrote, hiked, ate meals together in the evening, and enjoyed the culture of the beautiful city. On the day I heard the yelling outside, we were hosting our friend Tara, who was at a Spanish language class.

In response to the noise, I walked into the shared courtyard and found our landlord with bulging, bloodshot eyes and a bright red face yelling at Warren while his tiny wife threw herself in front of him to try to calm him down. The scent of booze was strong.

Warren turned to me and said, "He just choked me!"

Warren was a curious blend of shocked and furious, holding his throat and trying to understand why someone would come unhinged over a request to borrow two lawn chairs. Warren was also trying to control his temper because our landlord was an older man and obviously having some kind of meltdown that Warren walked into. His reaction was completely out of proportion to Warren's request, and we couldn't figure out why it happened.

We don't travel with a suitcase full of drama. We prefer to get our excitement from great experiences, not manufactured suspense. We've taken great pains to surround ourselves with positive people and cull the negative influences in our lives, so when one sneaks in under the radar it's shocking. We were immediately regretting the weeks of tolerating his increasingly strange behavior.

But this was where one of the key strengths of our relationship came into play. Instead of being drawn into the drama and mayhem like gut instinct would propel us to do, we made an almost instant decision to distance ourselves from the situation.

In the past, that wasn't always so. We used to both scold, using a breakdown as a teaching moment. "What did you expect?" was our standard line when disappointment happened. "I told you to do it this way, and you wouldn't listen." Can you imagine Wonder Woman saying, "you only have yourself to blame" before saving someone? It wasn't until we learned the "be the hero" strategy from our friends

Kent and Caanan that we finally earned our capes and became true heroes to each other.

As they explained it to us, in any relationship there are going to be outside stressors that mainly affect one person. This can be work, family situations, social obligations, or even while undergoing health crises or personal struggles. It isn't that it doesn't affect you both, but it doesn't affect you both to the same degree.

One of you sees it and possibly feels it, but the other one is *in it*. One of you can still choose to be on the outside of the situation, working to guide the other out safely. But without a little forethought, it's easy to get dragged into the drama, and when that happens you only make the problem worse. A lifeline needs to be tethered outside the danger zone, and the minute you leave your post, your partner has to find his own way to safety while worrying about you at the same time. It makes a setback that much harder to recover from.

In this scenario, it was my job to be the lifeline for Warren, to get him out of this situation and back to normal as quickly as possible. Seeing the red marks on his throat and the crazed look in the landlord's eye made me want to jump in with both feet, defending my partner like a lioness, but I remembered the advice about being a hero and strapped on my cape instead. Because if we both took a ride to freaky town, it would be a long road back to normal.

I told the landlord we'd be vacating immediately and I'd be back in an hour to get our deposit. We wouldn't be staying in a place where we were at risk of physical assault, even from an old man. As we walked back to our house, our friend Tara walked into this little *telenovela*. She was confused at first, but then she quickly rallied and began packing her things. She didn't add to the drama, and for that I was thankful (this is why it pays to surround yourself with great people).

Warren began packing our things while I went online to find us a new place to live. In every interaction with Warren I spoke in a calm but straightforward tone and told him I would take care of securing a new rental and getting our deposit back. He didn't need me to amp up the stress, even if I was agreeing with him. He also didn't need me to talk him out of his anger. We focused on logistics and facts, not emotions.

He mumbled and grunted and paced and did all the things you do when you're angry. And I let him, as long as he continued packing. I found a new rental just five minutes' walk away and called the owner. It was available, and we could move in that evening. I gave Warren the address details and asked him to start walking our bags that way.

As you would expect from his earlier behavior, my interaction with the landlord to get the deposit back was not smooth sailing. He tried a variety of tactics to delay me and keep our money and extend the drama. Instead of taking the bait or gloating over our new rental, I kept repeating the phrase, "I'd like to settle our business as we agreed" and "I'm interested in resolving this, not rehashing it." It was my job as the hero not to get drawn into the drama and instead work as the fixer to get us back to normal. The more talkative he got, the more calm I became.

When the landlord finally gave up on baiting me and counted out the money he owed us, he looked up, sighed, and said, "I'm empty." It was unexpected, and probably the realization at the end of his freak out that he'd made a bad move. After all, he'd just lost guaranteed rent at the start of the slow season. But it was hard to work up any sympathy for someone who used violence and intimidation as communication tools.

He told me he was mad that we were taking in rent from all our guests that should have gone to him. He thought we were running a hostel on his property. I was stunned.

"Why would we charge rent to our friends?" I asked.

He couldn't imagine that we'd invite friends to stay with us without charging them, because that's what he'd do. And since we told him we'd be having guests over the winter in this 3-bedroom house when we first rented it – and were paying all utilities ourselves – it never dawned on us that he'd have a problem. In fact, since many of them were travel writers and photographers, it would have been a smart move for him to play up the property in hopes of getting an online review or some professional photographs. But he looked at life through a negative lens, so it was difficult to see opportunity like that.

I shook my head as the light slowly dawned on him that he'd figured it all wrong. He next tried to play the sympathy card. He told me he'd just gotten some bad news that day and tried to go into detail about his problems. I again repeated that I just wanted to resolve our business and go our separate ways. I was Warren's hero, not his. Then he said I'd never find another place to rent on such short notice. Maybe we could work something out and stay? It was all just a misunderstanding, right? No thanks, mister.

Money in hand, I walked away from the drama and back into normal life. The whole thing was over in just over an hour.

Warren was waiting at the new house when Tara and I arrived, having just paid rent to our new landlord, a Mexican optometrist who screamed normal in the way our previous landlord did not. We instantly felt at ease, especially when we walked into the two-bedroom house and took the stairs to the flower-filled roof terrace. We poured some wine and toasted normalcy.

As we travel and run into challenging and sometimes difficult circumstances, we take turns being the hero so we can quickly get back to normal. The time for second-guessing and learning lessons is after the situation is over, when the angry old man has gone back inside and we are sitting on our new terrace, surrounded by flowers and tranquility.

24

The Great Train Robbery

We like to think our travels have earned us badges of respect. After tens of thousands of miles of travel by boat, plane, train, car, motorbike, horse and camel, we were pretty savvy about how to get along safely in this world. We considered ourselves experts, never having been robbed or pick-pocketed in three years of constant travel. All that changed when we took the train from Austria to Budapest.

The previous night was spent on a sleeper train from Germany, laying in our bunks and pointing out the occasional castle spotlighted against the dark sky before we drifted off to sleep. Nights on trains were usually enjoyable, and we'd had plenty of practice after riding across Asia and now Europe in them. That night we had the bad luck to have a snorer in our compartment, so we tossed and turned. *Oh well, things could be worse*, we thought. Little did we know.

As we yawned and stretched in the early-morning light in Vienna, our next train chugged into the station, stopping at our platform with a hiss. The doors opened and we boarded, finding two seats in an almost empty car for our three-hour ride to Budapest. It was a nice train, clean and fairly new, and quiet on this weekend morning. We stowed our big backpacks at the end of the train car, taking our daypacks with our valuables to our seats. Warren nestled his bag between his legs on the floor, and I opted to put mine in the rack above so I could stretch out my legs. The cabin was practically empty, so I didn't have any worries.

We hunched down in our seats to read and watch the scenery go by, as this was a lovely part of the world. Budapest was our last stop before our month-long hike in Turkey, and we were looking forward to the spas, the goulash, and meeting up with some American friends who lived there. The plan was to indulge in some luxuries like spa days and heavy Hungarian food before the difficult days of the big hike started.

About 30 minutes in to the journey, we stopped and four older ladies boarded the train with huge suitcases. We smiled at each other like we always do when people seem to pack everything they own for a short trip and it's still more than we require to live on the road full time. We got up to help them put their bags overhead and that's when we made the discovery – my daypack was gone.

In it were my passport, bank cards, driver's license, 3-month-old Macbook Air, iPod, camera, backup drive, and my favorite lipstick and lip balm. It had my sunglasses and my favorite scarf along with the high-end Columbia rain jacket that kept me dry during our trek in Scotland. I even had my flip-flops hooked on the outside. Everything I needed for the day-to-day, including our business, was in that backpack.

My gut clenched and my heart stopped. I frantically pawed around the suitcases Warren had just loaded for the older ladies, thinking it was shoved behind them. Nothing. Warren asked me what I was doing, and I clutched my shirt at the neck and told him my bag was gone. He ran to the window to see if anyone on the platform had it, mistakenly taking it when they got off the train, but the green and gray bag was nowhere to be seen.

I moved from compartment to compartment, looking in overhead bins, bathrooms, and trash cans for my bag. It was slowly sinking in that it was gone, stolen by a pro who sensed our inattention in the almost deserted car. My heart was beating out of my chest, pounding through my ears, when I finally admitted the backpack was no longer on the train.

The train attendant smiled sadly at my tale and told me it was a not-uncommon occurrence on trains going into Budapest. Thieves worked in teams to find unsuspecting travelers. One stood in front of the victim, putting his bag in the overhead and pushing it down the rack, forcing the victim's bag to be pushed behind her. Then another person picked it up from behind and walked away, never getting in visual range of the victim. The thieves then quickly and quietly got off at the next station. Had those ladies not boarded the train and needed help with their luggage, I wouldn't have known my bag was gone until we arrived in Budapest hours later. With shaky legs, I walked back up to our car to find Warren, expecting him to be furious with me.

When I arrived he was typing on his laptop. The train had Wi-Fi, and he was methodically changing all our passwords. "At least they didn't take your passport and credit cards," he said as he continued typing. I stayed quiet, wondering how to tell him I'd broken our cardinal rule of travel, the one designed to avoid the theft of our most precious possessions: we always carried our passports and credit cards on us on travel days. Credit cards and passports are the most difficult things to replace in a lifestyle like ours with no permanent address. So we guarded them carefully when traveling, knowing everything else was easier to replace. Or at least we usually did.

The night before on the train my money clip kept digging into my leg as I slept, so I emptied my pockets into my backpack and rolled over, intending to put them back in my pocket in the morning before we reached Vienna. But the snoring man in our compartment kept waking me up, and when we arrived in Vienna I was walking in an exhausted fog. It completely slipped my mind, and now I was on a train to Budapest with no identification, no credit cards, and no laptop. But I was definitely wide awake.

It was a rookie mistake to leave my bag unattended on public transportation, no matter how nice the train or how empty the car. I felt so dumb to be taken by such an obvious scam, something a veteran traveler should have known. I later Googled "travel precautions in Budapest" and the first hit was a warning to keep backpacks between the feet on public transportation.

When I told Warren my passport and credit cards were in the backpack, I expected an angry reaction.

After all, I had broken the rule, the one we agreed upon years before. And I'd just locked us in place in Budapest with no money and no way to leave the country. All our bank cards were joint, so when we reported mine as stolen his would be canceled as well. We were leaving for Istanbul in two weeks for a month-long hike we'd been planning for six months, but we couldn't go if I didn't have a passport and we didn't have access to money. We were stuck, and it was my fault. I felt like such a jerk.

To add to the drama, there were rumors of a U.S. government shutdown because politicians were fighting over the budget. If that happened, nonessential services like passport replacements would be shut down just like the national parks. I felt sick to my stomach, thinking of the money I'd cost us, the aggravation we'd have in replacing our credit cards in a foreign country, and the very real chance that our biggest trip of the year could be canceled because I wouldn't be able to leave the country.

Warren surprised me. He was visibly upset that I broke the rule, but instead of yelling or scolding me, he simply logged on to the U.S. Embassy website in Budapest and scheduled an appointment for first thing Monday morning. By the time we arrived in Budapest, all our passwords were changed and bank cards were canceled. Nothing he said would be a deeper lesson that what I was feeling, so he didn't bother. He held my hand when I started the ugly cry.

Our Hungarian landlord was a young woman named Helga. When we arrived at the flat to meet her and I told her our situation, she was upset. She didn't want us to think Budapest was dangerous or dislike its people, and we assured her we didn't. Bad guys live in every country, and there's no way of knowing whether the thieves were Austrian or Hungarian or something else altogether. I was still too busy beating myself up to blame the thieves. I felt so dumb, and I was embarrassed to tell anyone about it, even a stranger.

Helga walked us to the police station to file a report. I hated to inconvenience her like that, but there was no way we could fill out a police report in Hungarian. They told us to come back in an hour, so we stopped for goulash, realizing we hadn't eaten yet. Helga encouraged us to have a beer. I said I didn't think it was a good idea to have beer breath when we talked to the policeman in an hour. Helga said, "No, really, I think it's a good idea to have a beer. You're going to need it." She left to run an errand and said she'd meet us back at the police station in an hour.

As we ate our goulash and drank the cold beer, I couldn't get over Warren's calm demeanor. He's the planner of our relationship, and also the one with the quickest temper. He gets aggravated when things don't work like they're supposed to, and I definitely broke a lot of our standing rules that day. But he was almost cheery.

I asked him to explain himself, why he was taking this in stride and I was freaking out. It was like our normal roles were reversed. He revealed that this was the day he'd been dreading since we left on this journey back in 2010, the day we had something precious stolen. And now that it had happened, he realized how little it would affect us in the overall scheme of things. It was going to cost some money and aggravation, of course, but overall we were okay. He could finally let this years-old concern go.

Bully for him. I was still a nutcase.

A belly full of goulash and a cold beer later, we were back at the police station in the waiting room...waiting. The hard plastic chairs and echo-chamber of a room made it even more uncomfortable, our every comment broadcast loudly to the room.

Helga went with me into the policeman's office to file the report since she could translate. Warren stayed outside with the loud drunk people who'd just been brought in for fighting and tried not to get intoxicated from the air.

At this point I had no expectation of ever seeing any of my stuff again, and in my mind we were just filling out the report so I could get a new passport. At first I thought the officer was taking his time because he liked Helga, who was very pretty, but I slowly realized he was actually investigating this crime, reviewing train tables and trying to pinpoint a time of theft so he'd know at which station the thieves likely got off. He thought there was a slim chance I'd get my passport and non valuable personal items back.

It's funny, but I didn't really start calming down from the theft until we were in the Hungarian police station with the gruff officer who didn't speak English. Somehow going through the motions, taking action instead of just feeling sorry for myself, was pulling me from the gloom. And I realized at that moment how lucky I was that Helga spoke English, wanted to translate for us, and that we stopped by the police station on a relatively quiet day. Most of all, I was thankful I had a partner who jumped in to help without judging and without attitude.

The policeman and I began joking with each other through Helga's translation. He asked about our travels and I told him my little brother was a policeman in the U.S. He said police work was very different over here. When Helga told me the delay in processing the report was because he didn't have internet access and couldn't figure out the exact jurisdiction based on my time estimate without a paper train schedule, I understood part of what he meant.

I couldn't imagine my brother solving crimes without access to the internet, or even a basic Google search to find train times in an investigation.

After writing out a Tardis-like list of contents in my tightly packed bag, I joked that at least I didn't have any money in there. When Helga translated the officer's response, I was chastened. He said "It's all relative." What I had in my bag in possessions alone was a small bit of wealth to most Hungarians.

We left a little frustrated at the hours spent filing the report, realizing why Helga recommended that lunchtime beer, but we were more lighthearted than we had been at the start of the day. In the end we only had stuff to replace. We were safe, and we would recover.

Warren and I both still have too much of the American "do it yourself" mentality. We hesitate to ask for help from other people, and we often hesitate to ask from each other. Warren gets mad when he sees me struggle with something and wonders why I don't ask for help. It's not that I'm trying to super-independent; it really is that I just don't think to ask. I'm working on that.

The day the bag was stolen, I asked for Warren's help. He didn't yell or get mad at my mistakes and took the necessary steps to safeguard our information and money. I hated asking our new landlord for help, but I knew I couldn't do it without her. And later that night we met up with our friend Will, the American living in Budapest. When he heard our story of woe, he told us his niece was flying in from the U.S. later that week. Did we want her to pick up a new laptop for us?

Why yes, thank you, friend. Within a week of this disaster, we were back to normal: new passport, new bank cards, and new laptop. We beat the government shutdown by one day. But if we hadn't asked for help – from each other and from those around us – we might still be stuck in Budapest waiting for the backpack that will never be found.

25

He's Not Out to Get Me

"Don't use your fucking poles!"

I stared down the cliff of white, windswept rocks at Warren, who was as angry as I'd ever seen him. He stood on a large flat rock 100 feet below me, the turquoise blue Mediterranean Sea at his back.

"Why won't you listen to me, dammit? You're going to get yourself killed!" Warren yelled. A vein was throbbing in his neck.

My first instinct was to shout that those would be some pretty crappy last words if I did. But I've learned over the years to respect the intention of his feedback even when the style of delivery is lacking. Well, I've mostly learned it. He had a good point about my poles being useless, and even dangerous, in this steep descent over smooth rocks. My elbow and knee were still bleeding from slipping and falling backward on my heavy pack, and I was shaking from imagining how much worse it could have been if I had fallen forward.

This hike in Turkey proved to be more challenging than we expected. We had already endured a torrential storm on the cliff, and we were hoping for better weather ahead. Not only were the routes difficult, but the days were getting shorter as winter approached and we had to find a campsite by 4 p.m. each day to beat the sunset. Since we never knew where we'd find flat ground for camping, we became hyper-vigilant after 2 p.m. each day in search of flat ground. This descent down the steep, boulder-strewn hillside was both difficult and beautiful, but we had little time to ponder either. It was already after 2 p.m. and we were at least two hours from the bottom. My fall meant I was slower and more timid in the steep walk down, further slowing us. Warren's anger was reasonable because we didn't want to get stuck on this cliff when night fell.

Hiking is a great metaphor for relationships. One person's pace, habits, and ability to share the load impacts the other person. If one gets hurt, the other has to provide care or find help. If one runs out of water, the other has to share this precious resource. When one person is slow, it prevents the other person from arriving at camp on time. Everything you do when hiking together takes this into consideration if you're a good partner. You don't want to drag the team down, and you don't want your hike unnecessarily impacted by someone else's carelessness or lack of planning.

My poles were a safety crutch, literally. We bought them in the U.S. the previous summer in preparation for this hike. Neither one of us were sure we'd need them, but for 30 days of walking with packs we thought it wouldn't hurt to have the extra stability. From the moment I started using mine, they became a second set of legs. I imagined myself as one of those four-legged Walker machines from *Star Wars*, which is strange considering I hadn't seen the movie in 25 years. But a long walk like this gave my mind plenty of time to source random bits of trivia.

On most terrain the poles worked great, giving added stability when climbing or descending. They helped to keep pace with a slight tap-tap on flat terrain. But there were some spots where poles were dangerous to use, and this smooth boulder-covered hillside was one of them. The poles had metal tips to better grab into the earth and provide stability. When using the poles on smooth boulders, there was a feeling of stability, but it was not trustworthy. There was nothing for the pole to dig into. I still trusted it, even though the poles could slip at any moment. Putting my weight on the poles was foolish. But my fear inspired crazy acts in spite of logic. The poles had become my friends, the tools to help me overcome my clumsiness and lack of upper body strength. As an extension of me, they made me a better hiker. I felt safer with the poles, even when they weren't making me safe.

As a kid, I was a clumsy sort. Sports were never my thing, even though I tried team sports like basketball and soccer when I was in grade school. I was much more comfortable with my nose in a book or riding my bicycle, both solitary activities. I didn't want to coordinate my moves with other people because I could barely coordinate them for myself. I was one of the taller girls in class, way ahead of most in my growth spurt. Besides being clumsy, I felt awkward in appearance. For the most part, I just wanted to fade into the background when it came to sports and physical education. Still, peer pressure was strong, and when all the girls in my class began taking gymnastics, I begged my mom to let me, too. We didn't have a lot of money for extras, but somehow she found it. I showed up to class in my black stretchy leotard, the biggest girl in a room full of bendy natural athletes. At the end of the class term, I mastered the cartwheel and nothing else. Backbends, balance beam, and high bars were off limits to my uncoordinated body.

Over the years, this disjointed and clumsy feeling grew. I accepted the fact that I was not an athletic person, so I didn't play sports in high school or even dance (aided by fact that the religion of my youth forbade dancing). This lack of confidence in my physical ability was in stark contrast to the strong confidence I had of my mental ability. I accepted that I was uncoordinated just like I accepted I was smart, and I didn't do much to challenge either assumption for years. In hindsight, this was a poor decision. Assumptions needed to be challenged in order to see the world – and myself – accurately.

Warren, on the other hand, was a stellar athlete in school. His mom took him to sign up for Pee Wee football as a kid, and they arrived too late to get on a team. She and some of the other mothers were directed to the signups for the relatively "new" sport of soccer in the U.S., and this was how Warren's soccer (*futbol*) career began. His mom tried to keep him busy, especially after the age of 10 when a drunk driver killed his father. He went overnight from being a boy to the man of the house, a role he didn't expect to assume for another 20 years. Soccer saved him by giving him a positive way to release his anguish and rage, though it wasn't a perfect cure. He had boundless energy and appeared as a tightly wound coil, ready to spring at any moment. Warren found comfort in physical activity and stoked the drive to win in all areas of his life. He channeled his energy into sports and school, excelling at both. Even in his 40s, his balance and coordination were impressive. He moved like a cat, and I began calling him Tigger long ago for his physical energy and enthusiasm.

As we faced off on the side of the mountain, our two histories in relation to physical activity came to a head. Warren was clearly the better athlete, coordinated and logical, visualizing his successful descent like coaches trained him to do. I was convinced of my clumsiness and looking for any feeling of stability on the way down because I didn't have any comfort of my own. His physical confidence impressed and irritated me, and I cursed him under my breath. For years this issue played out in our marriage, his ability to just "know" how to do physical tasks and what I perceived as his impatience when I didn't follow suit. He thought I was just being difficult, stubborn and stuck in my own ways and unwilling to learn from him. We were both right.

But now we were in a situation where it could cause us harm. I'd already fallen once, and the ache in my thigh meant in addition to the blood oozing from my knee and elbow, I'd probably have a whopper of a bruise. We still had a long climb down and a camping spot to find before sunset, not to mention restocking our food. Warren tried a different tactic.

"You scare me so much you make me angry. I don't want you to fall, and if you don't listen to me you will fall again, only this time it could be much

There are the small issues, like how to best load the dishwasher or drive the car. And then there are the more difficult conversations, like how to tell each other when your health is sliding, you aren't working hard enough on the business, or that you're spending money foolishly. Those are hard conversations, but in a partnership they are necessary. Neither one of us likes being called out for making a mistake or not performing up to par. We don't want to be seen as lacking in front of the person we love.

During our travels, plenty of "opportunities for improvement" arose. We once even fought over the way we brought up problems to each other. He hated being the tour guide of our relationship, booking all the plans, and I hated being bossed around. He wanted me to take a bigger role in keeping us on track with our daily walks and health, and I wanted him to stop buying sugary snacks. There was always something. We continued giving each other feedback in order to be better partners, though we also nagged about inconsequential issues, like how I packed my backpack or how Warren was prone to spilling his drinks. It was sometimes hard to know what to bring up and what to keep quiet.

With our business, it got even more detailed. Even though we both had considerable business experience, writing books and working together was completely new, and we struggled knowing which way to grow. We began coaching each other on the ways we thought the other needed to improve, sometimes coming from a place of experience and sometimes from a place of irritation. It took some time to learn the difference between the two.

What finally took us from nagging to results was learning to separate our individual selves from our actions. Warren might do something dumb, but it doesn't mean he is dumb. I could write a crappy article or book, but it doesn't mean I'm a poor writer.

Feedback became separate from our egos. We imagined ourselves looking at the feedback from the side instead of from the center, totally removing our individual selves from it. Was it legitimate? Could we learn from it? Adjust our actions and have a better result?

By untying our personal worth from the feedback on our projects, we moved light years ahead in our relationship and our business. I'd like to say there's no more yelling or hurt feelings, but that's not true. Sometimes we yell, and sometimes we're jerks. But overall, we realize that the feedback comes from a good place, even if the method of delivery is not ideal. And when you know it comes from the heart, it makes it easier to take it to heart.

26

Who's In Charge?

The cava was chilling in the refrigerator, ready to celebrate the New Year at the stroke of midnight. A fire blazed in the hearth upstairs in the sitting room, and music was playing low through our laptop speakers.

Warren brought a tray of food upstairs: olives, cured meats, cheese, bread, and jam. The lights were off with just the glow of the fire to light the room. Our American friends Kent and Caanan were visiting us in Spain, and we'd spent the last few days walking along the *ramblas* of this sunny region and driving through the countryside.

We met Kent and Caanan in Seattle after first knowing them through mutual travel-loving friends online. From the first moment we met for coffee, running in slow motion toward each other on a cross walk, we've had a goofy and warm friendship. Conversation is deep, but always tinged with wit and humor.

route. At mealtimes, I made the choice between the selection of restaurants if there was no clear favorite. Warren didn't have to think about it. He could just enjoy the trip.

It doesn't sound like much, but these daily decisions were mind-boggling. So many small details to figure out. I liked having a say in the long-term projects in our life for work and travel, but this everyday stuff was not my cup of tea. I began to appreciate the role Warren had been playing all along.

Warren's role as copilot was equally challenging. As much as he enjoyed the break from leading our adventure, he was chomping at the bit to stay at it. He had a tendency to over plan things, to look at every possibly scenario. It bugged him that I didn't, and he wanted me to pilot just like he had all this time. He was uncomfortable with the supportive role, taking a backseat and working in the shadows while I took the spotlight.

It didn't help that we were soon in Morocco, where women are not generally the ones making orders in restaurants, asking for directions, or negotiating prices. More than one Moroccan told us that women rule the homes and men rule the streets. We never had the offer to go to a Moroccan home, so I can't vouch for a woman's power there, but we could certainly see the men were in charge of outside world. Warren had to step up more than once because I was culturally blocked from being the pilot in public.

We were unhappy in Morocco, feeling the constant pestering to buy every time we walked out the door (my friend! my friend!) and seeing a very male-centric view of life. Women were hidden from view, even in public through their robe-like clothes and scarves. The cafes were full of men, smoking and watching the world go by.

The weather that time of year was cool and rainy, keeping us inside much of the time. Our first apartment was too dirty, and even though we liked our second one, the oppressive nature of being a woman in that environment was too much for us. Of all the countries we've ever visited, Morocco is the only one I'd recommend a formal tour over independent travel. It's just too difficult for women.

As pilot, how much control did I have? We were with our friends, and I couldn't very well boss them around. We had all booked this month together with a specific budget, and I didn't want my decision to negatively impact their finances. Our biggest worry was that we needed to be out of Europe for at least a month, having run out of time on our visa.

Alison and Andrew deferred to me on whether to stay or go, and we began a negotiation. Warren was antsy because if it were up to him we would have just left, visa be damned. We finally decided to leave ten days earlier than planned. It was up to me to negotiate with our landlord to get some money back and figure out the ferry times. Thankfully Andrew spoke French and negotiated our early-morning cab plus the ferry.

I was beginning to learn that being the pilot didn't mean I had to do everything myself.

These roles didn't quite fit us, and given the environment we performed poorly. Warren kept trying to take the lead, and I kept focusing on the details like a copilot. When it came time to switch off in February, we both breathed a sigh of relief. We were back to our comfortable roles. But this time, it was different. I had more respect for Warren's role as pilot after trying to do it for a month, and I did what I could to make it easier for him. I stopped checking out of the process and thought of how I could genuinely help him. He became more appreciative of my supportive efforts as copilot after struggling with them himself. We decided to continue the experiment.

We had a Skype date with Kent and Caanan a few months later and they asked how we were doing. We had to admit some bumps along the way trying to figure out exactly what we wanted the roles of pilot and copilot to be, and they agreed it would take time and experience to decide. They also reminded us it was our choice as to what these roles looked like, as there were no hard and fast rules. Every relationship gets to decide how to balance the load of responsibility. Since we've left Morocco and been in more open environments, the roles are getting easier.

It's hard to deny what a relief it is to get my copilot role back every other month, but learning to take the lead in our life and relationship has given me a greater appreciation for what Warren has been doing every single day. And I like to think he feels that way about me, too.

Splitting leadership on a month by month basis is easier said than done, but it is a worthwhile effort in balancing the load of our relationship. And when we look to successful, long-term couples like our friends Kent and Caanan, it just makes sense to give it a try ourselves.

If we're going to keep going on this journey of love, we need to both be able to man the controls.

the kitchen to be a proper chef's workspace. We could imagine an enjoyable life both together and hosting our friends and family. In over 100 destinations thus far on our travels, we'd not had that feeling, so it was a pretty good indicator we were on to something.

We'd been talking for months about investing in a small property, a place to function as a home base. After living this traveling life since 2010, we knew we were never wanted to stop adventuring. But every place we looked at up to this point was either too remote, too expensive, or not a place we'd consider coming back to again and again over the years. This house had been 85% renovated by the current owners before they fell behind on the mortgage, eventually giving it back to the bank. It sat unloved and vacant for four years, waiting for us to arrive. It wouldn't take much to finish it off and move in.

The months of conversations about evolving our lifestyle and investing some of our retirement savings all came together the moment we saw that house and made it easy to say yes. One thing I've loved about our relationship was that we never had to wonder what the other one was thinking.

We knew what we wanted. We knew our budget. And we actively looked while patiently waiting for the right house to come along.

The house in Spain fit the bill. We looked at the house on a Friday and made the offer the following Monday. We went from nomads to ex-pats almost overnight. Like most of our big life changes, we were surprised at how fast it happened after we took action. We never dreamed we'd be homeowners again, much less in a 430-year-old village in Spain. Was it really only three months ago that we arrived here for a simple house sit?

The train pulled into the station in Almería, Spain at 9:30 p.m., and we were tired. We'd just spent 12 hours seeing Spain from the window of a train, starting that morning from Barcelona. We looked for the man who was supposed to meet us, the owner of the home and dog we'd be watching for the next month while he and his wife traveled to visit family.

Mike waved in greeting, a gregarious Scotsman with a fondness for jokes and puns. We loaded our backpacks in his SUV and drove off in the darkness for his home an hour away. Conversation flowed in the front between Warren and Mike, but in the backseat I was trying to tamp down a growing nausea. The winding roads through the hills were making me sick, and because it was dark I had nothing to focus on to quell the nausea. *Oh please oh please oh please* don't let me throw up in this man's car!

We arrived at Mike and Cheryl's beautiful home just outside the village and shared a delicious dinner together. By the time we went to bed in the cool, cave-like room, we were like the walking dead. We slept for 10 hours.

The next day Mike and Cheryl asked if we'd like to pick olives with them. We helped Mike roll out the mesh on the ground to catch the olives, and then we began combing through the branches with hand-held rakes to strip the olives from the tree. Thousands of olives fell into the mesh, and then we transferred them to large buckets. Later, we drove this treasure to the local olive oil processing plant. We dumped our olives into the processor, where they bounced on conveyer belts as they were stripped of stems and seeded to make olive oil. We left with five liters of olive oil, excited to be able to cook with some of it over the next month.

Mike and Cheryl hosted a small holiday gathering the next day before they left on their journey. Mince pies and mulled wine seemed odd in the warm Spanish sunshine, but we were excited to meet their friends and neighbors and hoped to forge our own friendships over the coming month.

One guest was a local real estate agent named Karen. Like he did everywhere we went, Warren asked her about the local market. Spain's economy had been in recovery for several years, and real estate was pretty much at rock bottom pricing. Karen patiently answered all of his questions, and Warren asked her if she would show us some property in our price range, expecting her to balk. Turns out, she did have a few fixer-upper houses we could afford.

That night as we got ready for bed, Warren told me about the appointment.

"I don't think we're ready for that yet, do you?" As much as we had talked about buying a place, one look at the large properties in the area we were in told me the price and maintenance here was higher than we'd be willing to give. I changed into my pajamas, thinking the subject was closed.

"It's okay. Let's just go see what's available. It won't hurt to look."

We met Karen at the local coffee shop on the following Friday, planning to walk to the houses on her list. (The village was that small.) The coffee was strong, and as we sipped Karen told us about taxes and the process for buying homes in Spain. I kept thinking this was a lark, that we were wasting her time and should have never made the appointment.

We couldn't afford a house in Spain, could we? And really, would we be happy in a tiny village? We're the people who couldn't stand living in the suburbs, remember?

As the morning wore on and we visited these quaint little houses on her list, we could see the potential in an investment here, both personally and financially. Our favorite ticked off all our boxes for lifestyle, price, and that "just right" feeling. We'd been talking about investing in a small property for months, but this was the first time it felt like something we wanted to do instead of something we thought we should do.

I had to admit, Warren had been right. We were ready for this. It's a little bit like love: when you know, you just know.

A few months later, after months of renovation and adjusting to the Spanish way of doing things, we moved in. The first night, we lay in bed looking up at the beams in the ceiling. We couldn't believe it was our house. The dying fire in the wood stove in the living room below radiated heat through the chimney running up the corner of our bedroom. We stayed warm despite the cool night air of the desert. In the shadows I saw the outline of my desk on the landing just outside our bedroom door, the village street lights bathing it in a soft glow from the window. I was going to create great things at that desk. We bought it from a local woman, carrying it down the street and up over the hill to our new house, stopping to chat with our neighbors along the way. All of our furniture was that way, second-hand pieces picked by us for character and comfort. Every piece told a story of where it came from or the person who sold it to us.

Warren cooked a white bean and chorizo soup our second night, christening the kitchen with a distinctly Spanish meal. We toasted with sparkling Spanish cava.

The local noises were still new to us: the garage door rolling up from the "everything" shop across the street at 10 a.m., the Scops owl that beeped in the night like a backup signal on a truck, and the sound of children laughing as they ran to their waiting parents at 2 p.m. every afternoon from the school up the street.

The house was everything we wanted and more, and I can't believe I ever doubted our place in this community.

Life in this small, whitewashed village in the hills of Andalusia is pretty charming. The weekly market falls on Wednesday, and it is here we buy our fruits and vegetables from the same mother-and-son grocers every week. The man who sells chorizo drives up in a vending truck, popping out the side canopy to do business. We always get a few links. Olives are a specialty here, and every week we have more than a dozen olive mixtures to choose from. After the market, people sit in the central plaza drinking coffee in the sunshine, catching up on the village gossip.

Warren has become something of a heartthrob among the older Spanish women in our village. He goes out of his way to say hello, engage in conversation, and even learn the local slang. He makes them laugh, and they pat his mane of hair and help him pick the best vegetables. It's sweet to watch him practice his Spanish this way.

Some nights we go out with new Spanish friends, starting with tapas and staying late into the night talking and joking with each other. Somehow, we all understand each other better after a glass of wine. It loosens up our inhibitions about saying words the wrong way and just lets us concentrate on getting to know people. But it isn't just Spanish friends; we're also meeting English, Scottish, Welsh, and Argentinean friends who've chosen to settle in this area.

Our neighbor is a retired tailor and brings us eggs from his hens. Another neighbor brings us oranges from his grove. We've even had a delivery of a jug of homemade wine to welcome us to this village. It's been overwhelming, a Norman Rockwell experience in a place 4500 miles away from the U.S.

As much as we love the quaint life in this village, we're not done traveling. In fact, we're celebrating the publication of this book by taking a six-week tour of Europe by train, visiting 10 cities and sharing famous love stories and romantic destinations in each. We're calling it an International Love Affair, because that's what our life still is.

At first we worried that owning a home would discount all that we had experienced before while traveling, changing our identities completely. But that's silly, really. Dreams aren't meant to stay static, or else we'd all still be that thing we wanted to be when we were 6 years old. Dreams are meant to change and grow as we do, and expecting things to stay the same is a sure recipe for disappointment.

We're evolving, figuring out what we want our everyday to look like, and then taking steps to make it happen. For now, this means owning a little house in Spain, living and writing here for up to half the year while we travel the rest. We have a bit more structure in our lives now, and with that ironically comes more freedom. We don't have to make our way from place to place with dead zones in between for working and writing. We can simply come home to Spain, recharge, and go back out again.

What will we do next? We don't know. The longer we live this lifestyle the less sure we are of anything except our love and commitment to each other.

Back in 2006 we were always going our separate ways, chasing our individual dreams and hoping they would match up. If we hadn't had that wake-up call at the Denver airport I have no doubt we'd be divorced now. We certainly would have never traveled the world or bought a house together in Spain.

Our travels have taught us a great deal about love and communication, and we're grateful for every lesson. But the single most important lesson we ever learned was to put our relationship first, to stop going our separate ways and journey this life together. It's a choice, and it took us a while to figure that out.

We don't know where our journeys will take us next or what we'll learn, but we do know we'll be in it together...at least for another year.

Afterward

Did you enjoy our take on love and life? The journey is far from over, and you can get weekly updates from us every Sunday on our insiders email list.

Find links to our weekly podcast about love and adventure, info on new books and courses, when we might be planning events near you, and all the funny, romantic, and scary moments that happen on our travels or in our quaint little Spanish village. Follow the romantic adventure at:

www.MarriedwithLuggage.com/Newsletter

Don't miss the preview of Betsy's popular book, Strip Off Your Fear: Radiate the Confidence Within. Just turn a couple of pages! But first...

Because we're indie publishers, we depend on readers like you to help spread the word about our books. Your reviews help other people find us in the huge online bookstores. Won't you take a moment to tell other readers what you think? You can find links to give reviews from all the major retailers here:

http://www.marriedwithluggage.com/thebook-spread-word/

Last but not least, please check out our other books at: www.MarriedwithLuggage.com/books. We're lucky to enjoy 4 and 5-star ratings from readers just like you on all of them.

Thanks for reading!

About the Authors

Imagine Spending Every Waking Moment with Your Romantic Partner.

Whether this thought thrills you to the max or chills you to the bone, you'll love the take authors and world travelers Warren and Betsy Talbot have on this extreme togetherness and what it can teach couples everywhere about shrinking the distance many couples feel as the years go by.

Through their website at Married with Luggage, Warren and Betsy have been testing their relationship in the public eye since 2008, when they first made the decision to quit their jobs, sell everything they owned, and travel the world full time.

It was a response to severe health crises in people they loved – people also in their 30s – that caused the Talbots to reexamine the hard-charging life they'd been living. They asked themselves the question, "What would we change about our lives right now if we knew we wouldn't live until 40?"

This powerful question prompted them to recreate their lives, their relationship, and examine the beliefs and habits that were limiting their happiness. It's also what got them one-way tickets to Ecuador in 2010, which started the life of long-term travel they enjoy to this day.

With action-oriented books, a popular weekly podcast, and revealing Sunday emails, they share the unconventional wisdom they've learned about living, working, and traveling together around the world...without killing each other.

They are the authors of *Dream Save Do: An Action Plan for Dreamers*, *Getting Rid of It: The Step-by-Step Guide to Eliminate the Clutter in Your Life*, and *Strip Off Your Fear: Radiate the Confidence Within*, all of which enjoy 5-star reviews from readers around the globe. They teach people how to let go of their past and make room for the present in their online multimedia course, Declutter Clinic.

Their latest book, <u>Married with Luggage: What We Learned About Love by Traveling the World</u>, chronicles their journey from the brink of divorce in 2006 to a rock-solid partnership today.

In 2014 they bought a house in a white-washed village in Spain, where they spend their time writing, walking the hills, and planning their next adventure.

Acknowledgements

This is the love story of two people, but it wouldn't be possible to share it with you without the help of many talented and generous people. First we'd like to thank our editor, Angela Barton, who made us sound smarter than we are. She's the reason this book isn't 800 pages of details you never wanted to know. Next, we'd like to thank our cover designer, Jacqueline Larcombe, who beat out dozens of other designers for the job in open voting among our readers. Talk about a tough gig!

It's hard to find honest feedback among friends, but we're lucky to have a few who will tell us what needs work and what doesn't. Many thanks to Akiyo Kano, PhD; Linda Rubright, Alison Cornford-Matheson, and Brianna Kietzman for providing detailed feedback on our earlier drafts. Your contributions made this book better, and we're grateful for your continued support of our projects.

Several other people brainstormed with us, providing great ideas for how to tell our story. Thank you Kent and Caanan Reiersgaard, Almut Gieseke, Karen Rosenzweig and Katy Woodworth (who knew that day we painted bodies and rode naked in a parade would get immortalized in print?!), Debb Whitlock, Andrew Matheson (who knows what the fox says).

A warm thank you to Mike and Cheryl Moran, who gave us the use of their lovely cortijo to write when our house was covered in plaster and sawdust.

From our writing community, the other indie publishers who shared advice, answered our emails, and generally showed us the way, thank you. Special thanks go to Sean Platt, Ingrid Ricks, and Kathleen Fordyce.

Last but not least, we'd like to thank our moms, Connie Gray and Patricia Ohlrich, who think we can do no wrong. It's your fault we've created this crazy life, and we can't thank you enough.

Sneak Peek: *Strip Off Your Fear: Slip Into Something More Confident*

Are you ready for a strong partnership? It starts with being able to say what you want and – more importantly, what you don't want.

"Speak up. Be proud of who you are, what you know, and what you do. Help other women do the same. When you change your world for the better, you make it better for the rest of us."

Betsy wrote *Strip Off Your Fear: Slip Into Something More Confident* for the "Good Girls" – women who go along to get along, never rock the boat, and put their own desires last.

Sound familiar?

In this book, she leads readers through a striptease of the emotional layers that can suffocate our innate confidence, preventing women from reaching their personal, professional, and societal goals.

In her signature style, she marries learning with action, using deeply personal stories to illustrate breakthroughs and then guiding the reader through exercises to reveal their own flawed and fabulous selves.

It is a bold book for women who want to live a life bigger than the one they have right now.

Turn the page to read an excerpt now...

Strip Off Your Fear

Fear

Radiate the Confidence Within

by Betsy Talbot

Author's Note

When I began writing this book I had no idea what kind of stir it would create. The more I shared about speaking up and owning our opinions and desires, the more other women wanted to know. Was I really going to say *that*? *In those words*? Yes, yes I am.

Amazing women came out of the woodwork to be part of this book and its message: women from their 20s to 60s; women with traditional jobs, volunteer jobs, and women entrepreneurs; heterosexual and homosexual women; mothers and childless women; those who are single and those who are partnered; women who live in cities and women who live in villages. The message of owning your voice and speaking your truth is universal and benefits us all.

There was one sticking point, however, and it was the term 'Good Girl,' which is used liberally throughout the book. While some women immediately identified with it, others shrank back or denounced it, stating it was misogynistic or demeaning. They didn't want to be referred to as any kind of girl, though most told me in very polite terms and said I was free to differ with their opinion and perhaps they were looking at it wrong. Ahem.

As psychotherapist Rachel Whalley said of the term: "Nothing captures quite so succinctly the role that all women in this culture have been taught to play. We don't want to be called a "good girl," but we want people to think we are just that."

If there is this much emotion wrapped around the term, imagine what it is like to live the definition every single day – choking on your own dreams so you can make everyone else happy. You can call yourself a good girl, a people pleaser, or even a wuss. What matters is not the name I call it in this book or you call it in your life but whether you identify with the definition and want to break free from it.

March 15, 2012

Chiang Mai, Thailand

Introduction

This book is for those of you afraid to be fully present, asking for what you want, going after the things that matter to you without pause or apology.

This is for those of you tired of being the Good Girl, the one who smiles to hide the clenched jaw, laughs off awkward moments, and takes what the world dishes out because you just don't know how to say no without disappointing other people.

This is for those of you who have insomnia or grit your teeth in your sleep because you stuff your words down all day long. This is for those who fake orgasms because asking for what you want is too hard and showing it is embarrassing.

This is for all of you who agree to do whatever someone else wants to do – dinner, entertainment, vacations, religion, political affiliation, lifestyle – because if you say what you really want you think you might lose your lover, spouse, friend, or family member.

This is for all of you who apologize for things you don't even do to keep the peace, clear the air, and maintain a balance.

This is for all of you choking on your dreams because you won't open your mouth.

You are scared because you are using someone else's voice, another person's words, and living another person's life.

This isn't you, and it never has been. You've been self-consciously adjusting this outer image, adding blister pads when it rubs the wrong way, learning to live with the constant irritation and resulting rash.

You think no one sees the real you, and you're right. You never give them the chance.

What would happen if you stripped off the ill-fitting skin of another person to showcase the delicious, full-grown, vibrant woman underneath? Would it ruin anyone else's life if you did this? Probably not.

Would it change your life? You're damn right it would.

Let's try it out right now while you're alone to show you how good it feels. Shut the door if it makes you feel better. Grab a notebook and a pen.

Now get comfortable. Take a deep breath and unclench your jaw. Relax your shoulders and welcome your thoughts, the ones you are scared to say in front of others, the ones you stuff down and try to ignore.

If you don't appreciate me, I'm leaving.

I want and deserve a raise for my hard work.

I've always wanted to do this, and this year it's going to happen.

Luxuriate in those thoughts, give them life, and welcome them. Step back and see them in the full light of day with no judgment. Walk around and examine them from every angle. Gawk at your audacity and nerve. Appreciate the complexity and nuances of your thoughts and the path it took to bring them into being. Capture them in ink in your journal. Don't worry about grammar and punctuation. Go with the feeling and let it *out*.

Put your pen down and read the words to yourself. Close your eyes and feel what you just read. See the words dancing on the back of your eyelids.

What you really want

What you no longer want (or possibly never did)

What you've been afraid to say

Now roll them around in your mouth for a while, tasting the power of having your words on the tip of your tongue, knowing you are going to release them into the world. Pull your shoulders back and say them out loud. Savor them as they come out of your mouth.

Say them louder; now louder again.

Your words, your feelings, your opinions are free. You've released them and nothing bad happened. In fact, you probably feel pretty damn good.

Go on; lick your lips like a satisfied cat.

Do you have more? Keep writing, even if you fill your journal or run out of ink. Read the words to yourself, close your eyes, and absorb every ounce of feeling for what you are about to say. Then release it into the room. Whisper at first if you need to. The feeling doesn't care, as long as it gets out.

What you need to be happy

What you want to accomplish in this world

How you demand to be treated

Tell the room what you've been dying to say for years about your relationships, your job, the food you like, the side of the bed you prefer, the places you want to go, your secret dreams, the way you want to be treated, and what you want from your lover.

Speak every single line out loud to yourself.

(Go ahead. I'll wait.)

Damn, girl. This is some powerful stuff.

Go on now; roll your head around on your neck a little. Stretch your limbs, crack your knuckles, and feel yourself settling in to your own skin, the one that fits like a glove. Make a little noise if you want. It feels good, doesn't it?

This is a small peek at what confidence and authentic living feels like. It is different from bravado or playing a part, because it comes from deep within. It isn't fake or put upon. It is real, as real as you are.

This book is all about uncovering your confidence and wearing it well, and we're just getting started.

Hold on tight.

Have you ever worn something that didn't fit? Maybe you gained a few pounds and those favorite jeans became a mini torture chamber, choking your legs to death and reducing your breathing to a quick gasp every minute or so. Perhaps it was a funky bra that gave you side boobs, or the jacket too tight to button but you wore it anyway because it camouflaged your ass. Did you cover it all up with a shapeless sweatshirt or muumuu giving no hint of curve, hiding all your womanly attributes? Maybe you pinched your feet into shoes that didn't fit or allow you to walk comfortably to portray a confident or sexy image you certainly didn't feel as you hobbled around.

We've all done it, and we've all paid for it. We don't look as nice when we wear ill-fitting clothing, and we certainly can't be ourselves, what with all the organ damage and suffocation going on. But we think we have to do this to get by, to cover up, to not appear to have gained weight, to look "together," or because we simply didn't take the care to buy clothes that really fit us to begin with. We're always adjusting to our environment instead of demanding it adjust to us.

It works the same way with voicing our thoughts, feelings, and preferences. We mash in our feelings and side boobs emerge. We flatten out our hungers and a muffin top peeks up. We cover it all with a shapeless tent of a shirt, hoping no one will notice everything going on beneath. We stuff, bind, elevate, squeeze, and mask ourselves to be presentable to the world, dying for the moment we can unbutton, unhook, and slip off our emotional torture chambers and just be ourselves at home.

But where is it? What is the "home" we long for, this place we can stretch out and fully be ourselves, loving our soft bellies, the slight jiggle as we walk, admiring our strong calves, broad shoulders, or breasts which nurture life and love? If you are a recovering Good Girl like me, this home is elusive. You are probably sleeping in your clothes, at least figuratively. We might laugh at characters like Tobias in *Arrested Development* who suffer from "never-nude syndrome," but there are a lot of people out there figuratively showering in their jean shorts just like him, terrified of seeing themselves in the buff.

Maybe one of those people is you.

This book is going to examine some of the ways we hide our true selves, silence our voices, and distrust our own instinct and judgment out of fear and uncertainty. I've told the story in the context of stripping off our clothes because this is such a perfect metaphor. Being naked is also not what Good Girls do. Until now, that is.

This isn't just an introspective exercise, however. After we identify all the ways we are covering up our true selves in the wrong costumes, we're going to do something about it.

We're going to strip off one layer of ill-fitting feeling at a time, unclenching your shoulders, releasing your breasts, emancipating your diaphragm, liberating your legs, and freeing your toes to actually grip the soft grass under your feet.

As we figuratively disrobe together, we're going to examine the fears and negative self-talk that taught us to cover, alter, lift, or compress in the first place and how we can confidently step forth in a mental and emotional outfit that actually fits our curves like a glove, showing the world exactly what we're made of.

How the book is arranged

Each chapter focuses on a specific body part to mirror an aspect of fear. It starts with a soundtrack for your emotional striptease and a few lines to tantalize you. If you want to listen to each song to get you in the mood you can find it on YouTube or download the entire playlist (https://c.itunes.apple.com/us/imix/stripping-off-your-fear/id509456916) for the book from iTunes. Then we get into the good stuff, learning how we got so covered up and, more importantly, how we can free ourselves.

Each chapter contains a special section to illustrate one of those pesky voices in your head, the ones who tell you to hide who you are and what you want. You're going to learn how to identify this gang of freaks so you won't be under their spell anymore.

The chapter is summarized with a section called The Naked Truth, and then an action sequence called Show Us What You've Got will show you how to put those lessons into practice on the main stage of your life. This is where a journal or notebook will be useful to help you explore your feelings and motivations as we work through your anxieties about self-expression.

Not everyone finds the same benefit from journaling, so I encourage you to explore and express in the way most beneficial to you. I find a lot of answers to my deeper questions when exercising outdoors or soaking in a tub – the "disconnected" states are best. The point is to give some time and attention to the prompts so you come away with a better understanding of how you first allowed yourself to be silenced by fear.

This serves three goals:

> To understand your past and how it informs your present

> To create your own path out of the silence

> To guard against allowing it to happen again

Why I wrote this

I wrote this book for the me of 15 years ago. At the time I had all these great ideas and energy but I pushed them down inside of me, waiting for some kind of permission to release them. It didn't even occur to me until I turned 30 that I was the only one holding myself back, and I spent the next 10 years of my life gradually owning my ideas and words and creating the life I always wanted. Since 2010, I have been traveling around the world with my husband after two years of saving and planning to live the life of our dreams (read more at: www.MarriedwithLuggage.com). Even though this is the thing people often find most compelling about my story, none of it would have happened without reclaiming my identity and voice 10 years earlier, and *that* is the story I want you to know so you can do it, too.

Books by people who skirt around issues and lay it on too easy are not for me, and I don't write that way, either. If I pick up a book to help me, I expect it to do just that in a clear and action-oriented way. My style is direct, and especially when dealing with fear and lack of confidence, this approach can be a little shocking at first.

This is your shortcut to the lessons that took me over a decade to learn. I want to put you on the fast track to living the life of your dreams – whatever that means to you – with confidence and power. These lessons are deep and hard-won.

By the time you finish reading this book, I want you to be in a delicious state of emotional undress, feeling the breeze and warm sun on the bare skin of your soul, the green grass of comfort cushioning every step of your life's journey, vowing never to cover your flawed and fabulous self again.

Now let's get naked.

To keep reading, purchase the full edition of *Strip Off Your Fear* in print or eBook format. Please visit:

www.StripOffYourFear.com

CPSIA information can be obtained at www.ICGtesting.com
Printed in the USA
LVOW13s2319210514

386781LV00005B/589/P